T0270075

Praise for *The End of Leadership As We Know It*

"Leaders are smart people, so if they're still falling short, we need to ask why. Garcia and Fisher usefully lay out the main traps that well-intentioned executives fall into. Only by realizing the traps—by recognizing just how appealing they are—can leaders avoid them."

—Erica Dhawan, author of *Digital Body Language*

"The rules for leaders have changed! In this gem of a book, Garcia and Fisher give you the keys to those new rules for greater collaboration and performance. They will teach you the importance of recognizing your people in meaningful ways, expressing gratitude, and to think about them more than yourself. Follow their advice and enjoy the journey!"

—Chester Elton, *New York Times* best-selling author of *The Carrot Principle* and *Leading with Gratitude*

"Don't let the book's title put you off. We need leadership as much as ever—it just needs to be more facilitative and supportive, less directive and centralizing."

—Garry Ridge, chairman emeritus WD-40 Company; the Culture Coach

"There is no one single leadership style that works in all situations—sudden, disruptive change requires versatility, the ability to change approaches to meet the moment. In this marvelous book, Garcia and Fisher identify the traps that limit a leader's versatility by over-relying on what worked in the past but can actually get in the way moving forward."

—Rob Kaiser, author of *The Versatile Leader*; president, Kaiser Leadership Solutions

"After 83 CEO engagements, I can say without hesitation that every board and chief executive I know is redefining what it means to lead in today's volatile and complex world. *The End of Leadership As We Know It* is a must-read—an enlightened reality check on the path forward for leaders all over the world!"

—Mark Thompson, *New York Times* best-selling author and world's #1 CEO coach

"Contemporary leadership is fraught with landmines and traps given the intensity and frequency of change leaders are faced with today. Garcia and Fisher provide a practical guide to help both seasoned and new leaders to sidestep these traps and thrive in complexity and uncertainty."

—Dr. Robin Cohen, head of talent management, pharmaceuticals, and enterprise R&D at Johnson & Johnson

THE END
OF LEADERSHIP
AS WE KNOW IT

THE END OF LEADERSHIP AS WE KNOW IT

What It Takes to Lead in Today's
Volatile and Complex World

STEVE GARCIA AND DAN FISHER

WILEY

Published by John Wiley & Sons, Inc., Hoboken, New Jersey.
Published simultaneously in Canada.

For general information on our other products and services or for technical support, please contact our Customer Care Department within the United States at (800) 762-2974, outside the United States at (317) 572-3993 or fax (317) 572-4002.

Wiley also publishes its books in a variety of electronic formats. Some content that appears in print may not be available in electronic formats. For more information about Wiley products, visit our web site at www.wiley.com.

Library of Congress Cataloging-in-Publication Data is Available:

ISBN: 9781394171736 (Cloth)
ISBN: 9781394171781 (ePub)
ISBN: 9781394171774 (ePDF)

Cover Design: Wiley
Cover Image: © takahiro/Shutterstock

SKY10050733_071023

To all the leaders who make their organizations and the world beyond a better place.

Contents

Foreword

Dr. Marshall Goldsmith

As an executive coach over the past 40 years, my mission has been to help great leaders get even better. As I've consistently found, what got you here as a leader won't get you where you need to go. That's especially true today, given how much faster and more complex the business environment has become. Today's companies face unprecedented challenges including geopolitical instability, pandemics, climate change, social media and disinformation, artificial intelligence, and the expected fruition of quantum computing. In response, successful companies are adopting new, more agile operating models, which in turn require leaders to change how they lead.

As any coach knows, relationships are the foundation for great leadership. That's how you build trust and collaboration both inside and outside your team, which are the keys to lasting success. Relationships are even more salient today, as companies seek to change how they work through a greater sense of purpose, the empowerment of employees at all levels, increased collaboration, and a culture of continual experimentation and feedback. Many of my clients immediately agree that relationships are the foundation for great leadership but are at a loss to understand how they can change these relationship dynamics in a practical way.

To address this dilemma, one of the principles I share with my clients early in our coaching process is to *stop adding too much value.* This bad habit can be defined as the overwhelming desire to add our two cents to every discussion. It's extremely difficult for successful people to listen to other people tell them something that they already know without communicating somehow that (1) they already knew it and (2) they know a better way.

Leaders often think they make things better by always trying to improve on ideas. They don't. Imagine that an energetic, enthusiastic employee comes into your office with an idea, which she excitedly shares with you. You think it's great, but instead of saying that, you say, "That's a nice idea. Why don't you add this to it?" What does this do? It deflates her enthusiasm; it dampers her commitment. The quality of the idea may go up 5%, but her commitment to execute it may go down 50%. That's because it's no longer her idea—it's now yours.

As a leader, it's important to recognize that the higher you go in the organization, the more you need to make *other* people winners and not make it about winning yourself. I asked one of my coaching clients, a former CEO of a large pharmaceutical company, "What did you learn from me when I was your executive coach that helped you the most as a leader?" He said, "You taught me one lesson that helped me to become a better leader and live a happier life. You taught me that before I speak, I should stop, breathe, and ask myself, 'Is it worth it?'" He said that when he got into the habit of taking a breath before he talked, he realized that at least half of what he was going to say wasn't worth communicating. Even though he believed he could add value, he realized he had more to gain by not saying anything.

Learning to become a trusted leader starts with the willingness to embrace uncertainty, the humility to change how you approach your team members, and the discipline to lead with listening first. *The End of Leadership as We Know It* perfectly captures how leaders start their journey into this new age of management that seeks to foster collaboration and creativity.

Steve and Dan have created a guide that goes beyond the surface-level principles and strikes at the heart of great leadership. Filled with stories and experiences—from the COVID-19 pandemic, to the war in Ukraine, to quantum computing—that will inspire you, their approach is practical and rooted in years of learned wisdom. Furthermore, unlike many others, they don't just recommend what to do. They advise you on what to stop doing, too. Often, letting go of old habits is the hardest part. You will learn to lead with heart, vulnerability, and empathy, to lean into curiosity, to focus on resilience as well as efficiency—and you'll transform the course of your career and business.

Become the leader of the future and watch your team, company, and relationships adapt and thrive like never before!

- Dr. Marshall Goldsmith is the *Thinkers50* #1 Executive Coach and *New York Times* bestselling author of *The Earned Life*, *Triggers*, and *What Got You Here Won't Get You There*.

Preface

In 1987, we sat in our respective college dorms listening to R.E.M.'s new album, *Document*. Lead singer Michael Stripe sang, "It's the end of the world as we know it." We could not imagine that 36 years later we'd find ourselves applying it to the radically different ways leaders today must navigate. Back then, we suspected that the advent of email and this thing called the internet was going to have an impact on the world, but we were too busy feeling fine to anticipate the destabilization and hyper-connectedness that was to come.

Early on in our professional paths, Steve in marketing and Dan in clinical psychology, both of us experienced personal earthquakes that changed the course of our careers. Steve was a young employee in the late 1990s as tech innovator Nortel Networks rose to prominence building the internet's infrastructure. A few years later the company, disrupted by nimble competitors, failed acquisitions, and corporate arrogance, melted down. His stock options evaporated, and he had a firsthand view as the once great company laid off close to 75,000 employees. The experience sparked his curiosity into what role systems and their leaders play in the success or failure of organizations.

Dan in the 1990s was a faculty member at Cornell Medical College, specializing in the treatment of trauma. In 1998, a team of executives asked him for a psychological consult. Their financial services company had just lost its leaders in the SwissAir crash over Nova Scotia. This encounter sparked his curiosity about how senior leaders and their teams can cope with loss, emerge from disruption, and optimize their performance as leaders, colleagues, and people. He began a new career in a field he hadn't even known was a viable career path for a psychologist.

Both of our careers grew out of disruption and destabilization. We emerged into the professional world after the Berlin Wall fell and as the digital revolution came into full effect. Like R.E.M.'s classic song, our world is frenetic, nonlinear, and, if we're being honest, at times incomprehensible. Current market conditions, popularly known as VUCA (volatility, uncertainty, complexity, ambiguity), mean that leadership as we once knew it increasingly leads to failure. In our work together, we have run toward the eye of the hurricane because we believe you often need to work through the turmoil to get to a place of clarity.

We share in this book what we've found: the principles and practices for a new kind of leadership that continually adapts to disruptive change. We also share plenty of stories, some with people identified only by their first name. In these instances, we've anonymized the example by changing some nonrelevant details, such as the person's personal information.

The two of us started working together helping clients in 2003. Eventually we helped build the first leadership and organizational effectiveness practice at AlixPartners, a global consulting firm known for helping companies navigate complexity and disruption. Being immersed with leaders and their teams at some of the world's most respected companies, such as Google, Boeing, Johnson & Johnson, Bank of America, Merck, Verizon, and Regeneron, we've had front row seats to the volatility and complexity that our clients increasingly wrestled with. The increased levels of ambiguity and uncertainty created by current market conditions challenge the traditional leadership practices that worked so well for many of our clients in the past.

Our curiosity into what leaders needed to do differently led us to cofound the Institute for Contemporary Leadership, along with our AlixPartners colleague Dr. Beth Gullette. Joining us was Dr. David Peterson, then head of leadership and coaching at Google and a leading thinker on how to handle rapid change and complexity. Since 2016 we have been working with a team of immensely talented consultants and thought leaders to study leaders, teams, and organizations as they wrestle with these contemporary challenges.

The stories and insights we share in this book come from both our experiences working with leaders and companies, and the many talented researchers whom we regularly interact with and learn from. Our hope is that at a minimum you will pick up hacks that better equip you to handle the increasingly difficult challenges inherent in contemporary leadership. If you're like some leaders whom we've partnered with, the behavioral shifts we advocate will be transformative for your work. You'll make a marked difference in the lives of your colleagues, employees, and customers.

In the spirit of R.E.M.'s Michael Stipe, we feel fine about the end of leadership as we know it. The world has indeed changed and companies and other types of organizations require new operating models, which in turn require new ways of leading. These include giving up the psychological needs to be the hero, to maintain tight control, and to be invincible. *Instead, it's critical to let go of the pipe dream of certainty, to lean into curiosity, and to build lasting influence by forging authentic relationships.* Inspired by the leaders you'll meet in this book, and the many wise people focused on refining operating models and leadership practices, we are optimistic and excited about the future of leadership.

—Steve Garcia and Dan Fisher

THE END
OF LEADERSHIP
AS WE KNOW IT

1

Introduction: Making a Difference in Our Complex Times

Jack stopped staring at the latest launch date estimate and put his head in his hands. For the first time he could recall, he felt like a failure. Worse, he couldn't figure out why. He'd been so confident when promoted to general manager of a division at the global medical device company where he'd worked for the past six years. But the playbook he'd used in his previous positions wasn't working.

Charged with integrating artificial intelligence into the division's products, he'd assembled a small team of trusted lieutenants to formulate a strategy. He then went to each group in the division to explain the strategy and make sure they understood their role in delivering it. Sure, there were some naysayers, but he'd expected that. It was a bold move. He had plenty of data to back up his plan, so he'd pushed ahead. After all, when the division hit its revenue numbers, everyone would benefit.

Eighteen months in, he was exhausted. He felt like he was doing all the work, making all the decisions, and getting involved in addressing every little issue. Even so, he was missing delivery dates due to data quality, and he'd recently lost some key employees, including the person responsible for the machine learning model. The CEO was impatient and frustrated. Jack had never been in this situation before. He didn't know what to do.

The End of Leadership as We Know It

In coaching and consulting with hundreds of leaders, we keep hearing versions of the same story: the practices and frameworks they learned in business school or from mentors no longer work. Many leaders are frustrated and anxious, wondering why they can't get their organizations to respond and execute as they once did. Their strategic plans keep getting upended by unforeseen circumstances. They conduct detailed analyses, build consensus, and execute accordingly, only to be disappointed by the results. In surveys, a third of these executives say they're extremely burnt out.[1]

This train wreck has been coming for a while. During the second half of the 20th century, big companies developed impressive structures and policies to meet a fundamental challenge: scaling up operations while controlling costs and developing marketable products. Technology was improving, but slowly and incrementally enough that most companies could take for granted the stability of their environment.

Since then, the ground has shifted. Digital technologies now enable almost instantaneous exchange of information, capital, goods, and even talent, creating a business landscape dramatically more connected than even a decade ago. Companies have used this connectivity to create new business models, from peer-to-peer (Airbnb) and streaming (Netflix) to cloud computing (Amazon Web Services) and cryptocurrency (Bitcoin). Yet such tight interconnectedness also leads to feedback loops and ripple effects that challenge traditional management.

No longer can leaders confidently determine cause and effect or predict the impact of any single change. Threats and opportunities emerge suddenly from anywhere and everywhere. Executives keep applying their tried-and-true models developed for stable environments and wonder why their efforts now fall short.

These trends have intensified in recent years, especially with the COVID-19 pandemic, pushing many leaders to a breaking point. Business thinkers have offered remedies, urging techniques such as acting more coach-like, establishing objectives and key results (OKRs), applying Agile methodologies, and adopting open-source principles. These are all good ideas, but they haven't enabled most leaders to lead effectively. Their organizations remain slow to react to outside changes, leaving them vulnerable to disruption or worse.

A big part of the problem is that leaders often don't know which of the proposed techniques to use, how to combine them, or the best way to adapt them to their own unique circumstances. It's been fashionable, for instance, to adopt OKRs to align team members on objectives, measure progress, and promote dialogue around what's working and what it isn't. We've seen OKRs work well in many organizations, but only if leaders fully integrate them into organizational life and couple them with other practices. Otherwise, the technique becomes one more quick fix that falls short. Peter Jacob, chief information officer at ING Bank, said it well: "What you can't do—and that is what I see many people do in other companies—is start to cherry pick from the different building blocks. For example, some people formally embrace the agile way of working but do not let go of their existing organizational structure and governance. That defeats the whole purpose and only creates more frustration."[2]

Leaders need assistance at a foundational level. To succeed in volatile times, they must first understand why their traditional approach—with its top-down hierarchy, annual planning cycle, and cascading execution—no longer works. With an understanding of what's broken, leaders are better equipped to address root causes. They can select the appropriate adaptive leadership practices, combine them to create positive feedback loops, and apply them in the real-world context of their own organization.

Leaders who take this comprehensive approach have indeed moved their organizations forward and increased resilience against unanticipated market shifts. They've responded quickly to threats and opportunities, retained talent, and positioned their organizations for future success—not by telling colleagues what to do, as Jack tried, but by equipping and orchestrating them in making things happen. Instead of doing the work themselves or trying to compel their workforce to change, effective leaders act as a catalyst and connector, getting people to initiate change themselves at the ground level in response to emerging developments. Everyone finally feels effective and part of a winning team.

Our Baffling Business Landscape

We can forgive leaders who grew up in the 20th century for wondering what has hit them. A simple example conveys the seeming randomness of today's business environment.

In 2020, the cereal giant Kellogg's hit an impasse with workers at its Battle Creek, Michigan, factory. Fourteen hundred workers went on strike, and the conflict dragged on for months. Then in November 2021, over 500 miles away, Sean Wiggs got involved.

Wiggs was just a student, a junior at North Carolina A&T State University. But he learned from Reddit's popular r/Antiwork board that the company had hired replacement workers. Furious, he fought back by writing a software program that inundated Kellogg's recruiting site with fake job applications. The program, dubbed *KellogBot*, turbocharged Antiwork's spam campaign. A video of Wiggs went viral. His and others' social media efforts appear to have helped encourage the company to offer concessions to workers and end the strike.[3]

Whether you are inspired or outraged by Wiggs's actions, the story points to the interconnectedness of today's economy and society. Companies face cascade effects and unintended consequences that prevent reliable forecasting because the system's parts interact in unanticipated ways. It's much harder to chart cause and effect, because the complexity goes beyond our analytical abilities. It's also harder to place bets, because what worked in the past may not work in the future. As a result, new opportunities and threats seemingly appear out of nowhere.

That's why executives who try to lead in ways designed for more stable environments find their traditional approach ineffective. Markets shift before their initial response fully plays out, leaving leaders struggling to formulate a new response. In the words of our friend and business agility expert Andy Czuchry, "Change becomes churn." Businesses are disrupted by the next wave of change, and exhausted by the prospect of having to react yet again. Many do not survive this cycle. Long-established operating margins have become volatile. Employees are burned out, due to unmanageable workloads and unreasonable time pressure. Even many of the largest, most established companies expect to be replaced.

At its core, executives' struggles result from a mismatch between traditional leadership practices designed for a command-and-control operating model, and our new fast-paced, interconnected reality. When the environment moves slowly or at a stable rate of change, a few people at the top of the hierarchy can decide on strategy up front, translate it into a set of objectives or priorities, cascade these down organizational silos for employees to execute, and then measure results and reward performance at year's end. They can discern cause and effect, and confidently plan for the future.

But today's environment is much faster paced and more interconnected. In 1930, for example, the half-life of an engineering degree was 35 years (i.e., the amount of time that elapsed before half of the knowledge a student learned over the course of their studies was superseded). Modern estimates suggest the half-life is now as low as two-and-a-half years: less time than it takes to earn the degree.[4] At the same time, international trade, travel, and telecommunications have all skyrocketed, increasing our connection to and interdependence on one another. As a result, small, seemingly insignificant events can have large and unpredictable consequences.

In this complex environment the traditional approach to leading organizations breaks down, for five reasons. First, up-front planning loses effectiveness as circumstances rapidly change. Second, cascading strategy not only increases delay but also limits the understanding of strategy by those expected to implement it. Third, organizational silos undermine the cross-functional collaboration now needed to address complex challenges. Fourth, a reliance on top-down communication inhibits the feedback needed to understand what's working and what is not. And fifth, the command-and-control approach reduces employee autonomy when it's needed most—to respond quickly to opportunities and threats on the front lines. The net result is a situation where a far-away programmer can disrupt management's carefully laid plans.

Embracing the Complexity Advantage

How can leaders manage this complexity? If traditional approaches are no longer viable, what's next? The study of complex adaptive systems offers some powerful suggestions. Found in the natural world, human societies, and increasingly in technology, these systems are dynamic collectives with multiple, autonomous parts that self-organize to address new conditions. They can sense and respond to those conditions, enabling them to adapt effectively to rapidly changing environments. Although not as efficient as hierarchical systems, complex adaptive systems are far more resilient amid volatility and uncertainty. Leaders who move their rigidly efficient organizations in the direction of complex adaptive systems will prosper in the future.

The study of complex adaptive systems offers four operating principles for thriving in unpredictability. Figure 1.1 identifies these adaptive principles as well as their traditional, command-and-control counterpart.

The first principle is rapid test-and-learn cycles versus up-front planning. Command-and-control leadership views strategy and execution as separate activities. This plan-and-do approach assumes that we understand cause and effect and can predict outcomes. We can therefore determine which activities will create value in advance and then task our employees with executing.

In fast-paced, complex environments like the Kellogg's strike, it's much harder to understand causality or to forecast. Advance planning becomes difficult, if not impossible, because circumstances are apt to change. Even the best strategic plans can become obsolete

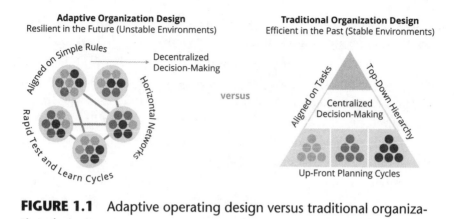

FIGURE 1.1   Adaptive operating design versus traditional organization design

before they're executed. Hence the finding, already back in 2015, that two-thirds of surveyed large-company CEOs said their organizations struggled to execute strategy.[5]

Instead of planning and then doing, complex adaptive systems conduct rapid test-and-learn cycles through continual interaction with their external environment. They essentially treat strategy as a hypothesis, or set of assumptions, that is continually tested and refined through action. In practice, this moves an organization from annual strategic planning cycles to much more frequent (quarterly or monthly) test-and-learn cycles. Agile sprints represent one way to put this into practice. By integrating strategy and execution, organizations move from plan-and-do to sense-and-respond. We like to call this *strategic doing*.

A second operating principle is to align on simple rules versus defined tasks. Stable environments not only allow leaders to plan in advance but also to translate their plans into tasks, and communicate those tasks down the hierarchy for the appropriate function to execute. These instructions tell employees what's important and how to interact with other groups. However, in complex environments, in which circumstances continually shift, relying on predefined tasks risks directing employees to pursue outdated goals.

Instead, complex adaptive systems use simple rules to govern behavior and interactions among the system's parts. When followed by the system's individual parts, simple rules, can result in surprisingly sophisticated outcomes without central coordination. In Atlanta, for instance, 370,000 drivers navigate road hazards, traffic conditions, and weather to get to and from work every day. They do this by following simple rules, such as driving at a certain speed and maintaining a safe distance from other vehicles.

Companies often communicate simple rules through organizational purpose statements, cultural norms, or heuristics such as Google's 10x thinking (employees should look for solutions 10 times better than anything out there). Organizational members use simple rules as guardrails to inform their decisions, guide their actions, and coordinate interactions with others. In essence, simple rules act as standards that govern everyone's behavior and promote collaboration by establishing norms and setting expectations.

As we describe in Chapter 5, the leaders of IAG, Australia's largest general insurance company, responded to devastating wildfires by changing the company's purpose from managing risk to making the world a safer place. The simple rules that resulted had a dramatic impact on how employees worked and equipped them to make decisions independently on behalf of customers. As a result, the company thrived.

The third operating principle is to decentralize decision-making. Simple rules by themselves don't help unless employees are empowered to apply them. Command-and-control approaches concentrate decisions at the top of the pyramid. That works in stable environments with plenty of time to make decisions; employees lower down in the hierarchy can escalate whenever they are unsure of what to do.

In complex environments, however, change is constant. As a result, small delays get compounded, which can ultimately spell disaster. Complex adaptive systems mitigate this challenge by distributing control. Like a flock of sparrows, Wikipedia community, or living organisms in a forest, any part of the system can influence the rest. This decentralized approach speeds action by enabling individual members to make decisions on their own, boosting flexibility and resilience by eliminating choke points.

Leaders in organizations can foster decentralized decision-making in different ways. One is through delegation. Another is by actively seeking employee involvement in decision-making. A great example of this is IBM's Red Hat division. Founded as an independent company with the belief that open collaboration was the best way to create better software faster, Red Hat naturally sees employees as an important source of insight and feedback. According to DeLisa Alexander, Red Hat's former chief people officer, "We don't legislate, we discover."[6]

One way Red Hat tapped into employees' ideas is Memo-List, an internal email list to which all employees subscribe. Former CEO Jim Whitehurst said he reviewed employees' posts to Memo-List daily and estimated that three-quarters of employees used the platform regularly. Memo-List gave employees a chance to express thoughts, ideas, and opinions. True to the values of open source, the best ideas rose to the top. As time passed, Memo-List became a vital platform for strategic conversations and a crucial element in the culture of meritocracy, which observers credit with contributing to Red Hat's repeated position on *Forbes*'s list of "The World's Most Innovative Companies" and Glassdoor's list of "Best Places to Work" as well as the company's acquisition by IBM for $34 billion.

The fourth and final principle is to organize around networks versus top-down hierarchy. Traditionally, organizations managed performance vertically, in silos. Leaders at the top of the pyramid told each division or function what to do, and managers in each area then directed employees' efforts accordingly and rewarded them based on their performance. Not surprisingly, employees ended up identifying with and aligning themselves around the priorities assigned to their unit rather than those of the broader enterprise.

Today, most work happens not in silos but horizontally, requiring collaboration from teams across the enterprise. Indeed, in today's business environment, it would be hard to find a value stream map that doesn't cross multiple functions. Solving complex business problems invariably requires that companies integrate diverse sets of experience and expertise.

Complex adaptive systems address this need by using networks to communicate and coordinate behavior. Networks are, in fact, the sole method of organizing in the natural world. Moreover, the configuration or pattern of the relationships within a complex adaptive system is dynamic—the system can rewire itself in real time in response to external stimuli. This is a huge advantage as the structure of the relationships between the system's parts, at least as much as the characteristics of the parts themselves, determines the system's performance. This is one reason many experts now define leadership not by a set of capabilities, but as a relationship.

In the past, most organizations didn't see or appreciate their networks of internal relationships. Additionally, if they wanted to change these networks, they had to restructure reporting lines, reengineer business processes, or redesign office space, all of which were both costly and slow. Fortunately, in recent years, organizational network analysis has emerged as a tool to uncover and analyze these connections. Applying this approach, leaders can modify how people interact and collaborate, creating faster, higher-impact, and more adaptive organizations.

One consumer health care company provides a compelling example of the power of cross-enterprise networks. By some estimates, a third of a consumer's purchase decision is based on a product's packaging. Accordingly, the company sought to develop innovative packaging to stimulate demand. Yet initial attempts proved disastrous. In one instance, the plastic required to create a uniquely shaped bottle interacted with the formulation, causing the bottle to shatter when dropped. The result was millions in wasted inventory, product launch delays, frustrated retail customers, and internal finger-pointing.

Dennis, a senior R&D director, was tasked with "fixing the problem." He soon realized that every department had a different point of view on what made for good product packaging. Marketing wanted the package to be attractive to customers, manufacturing wanted to make it reliably at low cost, and R&D wanted it to protect the product it contained. It wasn't that any function lacked expertise. It was that the functions didn't understand each other's perspective and weren't interacting. Siloed thinking was causing the problem.

To overcome the siloes, Dennis brought everyone together, having each function share their perspectives and suggest improvements to the larger team. As participants started to understand each other's point of view, they forged new relationships. After a series of meetings, a consensus emerged, and the group agreed on a new approach to design. Having gotten to know each other, they stopped the finger-pointing. When people had a concern, they picked up the phone and called each other directly. Collaboration soared, and suddenly problems were getting solved. The time to develop new packaging was reduced by 25%, and the team calculated that the approach would generate $70 million in incremental revenue.

Complex Adaptive Systems in Wartime

The advantages of these operating principles over traditional command-and-control approaches were apparent during the first year of Russia's invasion of Ukraine. As we write this in early 2023, the war is far from over, but many observers judge the invasion to have failed on multiple levels. When Russian President Vladimir Putin launched the full-scale attack on the much smaller Ukraine in February 2022, he anticipated a rapid and decisive victory, one that would secure his place in national history. Instead, Russia has suffered tremendous losses, its economy is in decline, and the Western democracies he sought to divide have united against him.

Many experts attribute Ukraine's success to differences between Ukrainian and Russian command structures. Ukrainian forces regularly test and learn (principle 1). They rapidly change tactics and create "MacGyver" solutions as problems arise.[7] They've modified Western missiles for MiG-29 fighter aircraft, adapted off-the-shelf drones to carry hand grenades, and repurposed Russia's abandoned and damaged armored vehicles.

By contrast, the Russians continued to execute the same, unsuccessful plan over time. In the words of one former US Marine fighting in Ukraine, "The Russians have no imagination. They would shell our positions, attack in large formations, and when their assaults failed, do it all over again."[8] Similarly, US Army Lt. Gen. Ben Hodges wrote, "Aside from moving ammunition back, I'm not seeing them being an adaptive force able to learn and adjust. I don't see any evidence that they have learned and fixed the things that were broken."[9]

Part of Ukraine's success stems from a shared purpose—expel the invaders—that energizes Ukrainian forces. While many Ukrainians volunteer to fight, more Russians have fled the country than reported to duty during Russia's late 2022 mobilization. Ukraine's common purpose acts as a simple rule (principle 2). It clarifies the priority (resist and degrade the invasion), fosters coordination across military units, and enables lower-level officers to act autonomously. Meanwhile, in the absence of a clear mission, Russian forces are left to blindly follow orders.

The application of simple rules, in turn, enables the Ukrainians to decentralize decision-making (principle 3). Junior officers make battlefield decisions, enabling their forces to capitalize on changing circumstances. By contrast, Russia's centralized decision-making means orders trickle down the command chain from Moscow, and frontline troops take little initiative.[10] Numerous Russian generals have died because of their need to be on the front lines telling troops what to do.

Finally, Russia's top-down hierarchy discourages feedback and disagreement. The result is an echo chamber in which leaders believe their own propaganda. Simultaneously, silos within the Russian military have made it difficult for separate units to communicate and coordinate operations. It now appears that hostility is bubbling up between Russian divisions. This social fragmentation extends beyond just the military. Russia has become a pariah with few friends in the international community willing to provide support in its time of need.

By contrast, Ukraine's military acts like a dynamic network (principle 4). Stories abound of drone operators, reconnaissance teams, intelligence officers, artillerymen, and paratroopers communicating over the internet and encrypted radios to coordinate their attacks and exploit Russian weaknesses. And Ukraine's network extends far beyond the military. Civilians from every walk of life have pitched in to provide support and resources, and President Volodymyr Zelensky has galvanized an international cohort of donors to provide military and financial aid.

The Ukrainian and Russian approaches couldn't be more different. As described by Suriya Evans-Pritchard Jayanti, nonresident senior fellow at the Atlantic Council, "Ukraine's aptitude for teamwork and ability to rapidly change tactics are factors that [Putin] simply has no answer for."[11]

Navigating This Book

Throughout history, enterprises have adapted their approach in response to changing circumstances. After World War I, with a surge in demand for manufactured goods, companies diversified to foster economies of scale; hence the multidivisional form pioneered by leaders such as Alfred Sloan of General Motors. This approach combined decentralized management with coordinated financial management. Forty years later, as a result of President Kennedy's ambitious vision to put a person on the moon, NASA revamped its unit-based leadership approach to program management and created the matrixed organization. Now even matrix leadership is still too hierarchical and slow.

Recognizing the need to change, even with a new path charted, doesn't make it easy. As leadership expert Marshall Goldsmith noted in his seminal book, *What Got You Here Won't Get You There*, leaders must unlearn what has worked for them in the past. In many cases they must act against their instincts.

We've written this book to help leaders make this transition. Others have advised leaders about disruption, complexity, volatility, organizational transformation, and related topics for several years. But none to our knowledge have offered a holistic approach that presents the spectrum of leadership practices now required for success and ground them in how organizations must operate going forward (see Figure 1.2).

Because of this gap, leaders have adopted tactics piecemeal, without understanding their importance, how each relates to others, or how to adapt them to the specific context of their own organization. Leaders haven't internalized what it *really* means to lead teams and organizations in an era of rapid and constant change. This failure proves especially damaging for leaders who think they're responding adeptly to market shifts, when in fact they're only wasting valuable time.

To address the gap, we share the *10 biggest traps* leaders fall into when leading in disruption, and what to do about them. Each of the next 10 chapters describes a mistake that leaders commonly make, often because they were simply following what they had been taught or what had worked in previous generations. Leaders don't have to rise to all of these challenges at once. But if they understand the main traps they'll face; how these issues can hurt them, their teams, and their organization; and how to overcome them, they're in a much better position to make positive change. As leaders focus over time on navigating specific traps, they can

Faster, More Complex
Business Environment

An inability to understand
cause and effect or predict
outcomes demands a new
approach.

Adaptive operating model
enables organizations to
thrive amidst disruption.

Adaptive Operating Model
Based on Principles of
Complex Adaptive System

Bringing the adaptive
operating model to life
means leaders must act in
new ways.

New leadership practices
create the conditions
needed to support the
adaptive operating model.

10 Leadership Traps
That Must Be Overcome

FIGURE 1.2 Holistic approach

embrace new strategies and tools in a holistic way, better responding to our age of complexity.

Chapter 2 addresses the tendency of leaders to neglect relationships in favor of building up their own skills and knowledge. It's easy to forgive leaders for falling into this trap. Historically, we've defined leadership as a set of individual traits or behaviors. However, in today's disruptive business environment, no one can go it alone. Those that try often end up wondering why they can't make things happen. Instead, leaders need to build and continuously tune a network of relationships that can help them collaborate, influence, and innovate. This relational view of leadership has profound implications for how we think about leader effectiveness. By shifting the focus from the individual leader to the leader-follower relationship, we can better understand the complex dynamics at play in leadership and create more effective and resilient organizations. Leaders who recognize the importance of relationships and act accordingly are much better positioned to succeed in rapidly changing, complex environments.

Chapter 3 builds on this discussion by exploring a trap that undermines leaders' ability to build strong relationships: the belief that leaders must avoid showing vulnerability in favor of demonstrating confidence. Too many executives believe their effectiveness depends on showing mastery over a situation. That made sense in earlier decades, when industries and competition were fairly stable and boundaries were clear, and when leaders could figure out the "right" answer and then rely on their positional power to get others to execute. The main leadership challenge was to gain authority; once you achieved the role, you could expect follow-through. But with most work now happening across versus within organizational silos, leaders today can't rely on their positional power. They must do the full work of influencing people and convincing them to follow a strategy. Leaders willing to express vulnerability build trust, enabling them to better influence, and create space for, others to contribute. As it turns out, colleagues appreciate a leader for being "real" or "down to earth," not projecting a false front.

Chapter 4 switches gears and challenges the conventional wisdom that leaders should separate strategizing from executing. We've all been taught to analyze market conditions and the organization's core competencies to formulate upfront strategic plans that in turn define the organization's direction, allocate resources, and determine priorities. But in today's rapidly changing environment, setting strategies up front can be a trap. Environments don't stand still while organizations perfect and cascade their plans. Consequently, most strategies are outdated before they're fully executed. Far better to combine the two steps—strategizing and executing—into strategic doing, where the strategy is a hypothesis continually tested and refined through experimentation.

If leaders are not setting strategy in advance, then how do employees know what to do? What prevents the organization from descending into chaos? The answer, in part, is the development of shared purpose supported by simple rules. Too many leaders get away with paying lip service to organizational purpose. They write about it in annual reports and other communications, but it is mere window dressing. As a result, employees have to look to leaders to tell them what to do.

Chapter 5 explores this trap. It describes how leaders can bring their organization's purpose to life and use it to create structures that empower and equip employees to act autonomously, as well as to inspire them by connecting their work to the organization's mission.

With employees able to act more independently, leaders need to let up some control. This can be challenging for those used to assuming command. Chapter 6 describes the traps leaders can fall into when they heroically take charge rather than enlisting colleagues. Most leaders learned to be effective by boldly committing resources and swooping in to fix problems, actions that are highly gratifying to the ego. But complexity undercuts that heroism by removing the predictability it requires. You might end up heroically fighting a battle that's suddenly moved to another place. Heroism also tempts leaders to focus on overt, spectacular stretch goals that capture everyone's imagination but may not fit what the company needs.

Enlisting colleagues, though, means that leaders must be open to others' feedback even when it challenges preconceived notions or established strategies and plans. Many leaders have been taught that such pushback represents resistance and it's the leaders' job to overcome it. Not only does that stance rob leaders of valuable information and undermine employees' engagement but also it reduces the organization's ability to adapt to disruptions. Chapter 7 delves into this trap and shares how leaders can work with colleagues' resistance to foster organizational transformation. Dissent, it turns out, helps stabilize the organization, which, surprisingly, is critical to adaptability. The most adaptive organizations are poised at the "edge of chaos"—between stability and disorder. Leaders don't need to overcome resistance so much as balance the organization between change and the status quo.

Chapter 8 explores how leaders fall into the trap, particularly in lean times, of promoting efficiency at the cost of resilience. Leaders today face pressure not just from investors and fellow executives but also from their own internal bias for efficiency developed as they move up the hierarchy. After decades of promoting operating efficiency, many leaders have been blindsided by complexity. We see this tendency most glaringly in the call to reduce inventories and eliminate redundancy. But within limits, redundancy creates space for innovation, helps diversify risk, and buffers shocks. Companies that remove all waste risk becoming brittle, susceptible to the first big disruption that comes along.

Chapter 9 describes the certainty trap, leaders' inclination to seek certainty rather than embrace curiosity. Leaders, similar to all human beings, crave stability and control. Moreover, people expect leaders to have the answers, and leaders respond by imposing certainty to contain everyone's anxiety. They think that engaging people means giving them confidence, but that's a shallow engagement, and the increased rate of change makes certainty a pipe dream. It's far more adaptive to stay curious, but harder psychologically for leaders. In this chapter we lay out techniques to make it easier.

Related to this preference for certainty is a tendency on the part of many leaders to rely on data for decisions. As we argue in Chapter 10, data isn't a panacea and is too often misused. We've seen how leaders use data as a front for a narrow agenda that would never make progress in full daylight. We understand the basic temptation: leaders are desperate for an anchor, and data seems wonderfully precise and scientific. But in disruptive contexts, data can be a trap that leads to delayed and outdated decisions that lack the emotional resonance needed to influence others.

In the same vein, Chapter 11, describes the traps that leaders fall into when they rely on external "best" practices rather than customizing their own approach. Best practices makes sense when you can discern cause and effect and connect your challenges with general frameworks. But in complex environments every situation is unique. Leaders need something specific and tailored to their company's circumstances. In today's complex world, the general framework will mislead or distract you from what's coming. Or it will push you to do what everyone else is doing, eroding your differentiation in the marketplace.

Finally, Chapter 12 briefly concludes the book with reflections on the future of leadership, especially in light of technological advances.

To understand the paradigm shift that we believe leaders need, it's best to read the chapters roughly sequentially, because they build on each other—especially the foundational first two chapters. After that, it's certainly fine to focus on the specific trap or problem that most challenges you.

Together, these traps cover the range of leadership struggles that we've seen in our work. *The End of Leadership as We Know It* can serve as a guidebook, but we think it's more than that—a new approach to leading organizations.

2 It's Not About You

Ivan Berg, vice president of Verizon's Business Group, now makes a point of staying in touch with colleagues. But when he joined the company in 2002, he didn't think about relationships. Initially he kept his head down, focused on developing his expertise, and relied on his supervisors to serve as his advocates. Fortunately for him, he got the wake-up call early. His manager and that manager's manager suddenly left the company, one on the heels of the other.

"Looking around," he remembers, "it was the most alone I've felt. My support structure just disappeared. It was really humbling. I realized I hadn't built any relationships outside my chain of command."[1] At the time, he worked in service delivery as the customer interface for new enterprise customers.

Berg knew he had to rebuild his network. He started by mapping out all the internal teams involved in activating a new enterprise account. He met with colleagues in orders, engineering, site survey, construction, provisioning, and field tech. All of them were relevant to his work in shepherding companies as they started up with Verizon service, but he hadn't spent any real time with them.

"I was humble and nosey because that's how you learn," says Berg. "I asked how they did what they did." After building a new set of internal relationships, he applied the same approach with customers, suppliers, and even competitors. Berg started to treat staying in touch with people as part of his job.

That relationship-oriented approach paid off over time, both for Berg and Verizon. At an all-hands meeting of the company's 300 senior leaders, for example, Berg stopped by to say hello to Mark, a former boss. Mark was huddled with his team working furiously to resolve a network outage for a large enterprise customer. Although the outage was the result of a fiber cut in the network of a Verizon competitor, the customer had called Verizon for help.

Mark asked Berg if he knew anyone at the competitor. Berg pulled out his phone and called a VP he knew there, who immediately promised to get a crew to fix the cut, prioritize the customer's two fibers in the 1000 fiber cable, and keep Berg informed on what was going on. Mark was amazed. "You got through in five minutes and we couldn't get in touch with anyone over there for the last hour," he said. Those connections boosted Berg's credibility in the organization, made Verizon look good, and got a Fortune 500 customer back online.

Networks Not Hierarchy

Berg's story highlights the trap of neglecting relationships within companies. Definitions of leadership have long focused on individual characteristics. These describe leadership as a set of traits such as creativity, charisma, and courage, and behaviors such as setting a vision and strategy, communicating effectively, and managing change. From this perspective, leadership is about the individual (the I), rather than the relationship between people (the We).

In stable environments, this competency-based view makes more sense. After all, if the conditions are steady, companies can optimize business processes and reporting relationships between employees for the firm's specific setting. The organization chart then determines how employees work together and who is in charge. What matters is what those leaders know, how they act, and the decisions they make. Except for those with external-facing roles, which are typically in greater flux, leaders can follow Berg's initial habits and pay little attention to building a broader set of relationships.

In an increasingly complex world, however, none of us, even with the help of the teams we formally lead, can meet all organizational challenges and objectives. We must turn to people across, and even beyond, our company for information, insight, guidance, assistance, and motivation. Similar to Berg, reaching out to the right person is often key to success. And rarely does a singular figure fulfill all our needs. The expert who harbors critical information probably won't be the trusted personal advisor or confidant to turn to with a sensitive problem or the influencer who helps rally people together. We must rely on multiple connections to gain the expertise and support necessary to accomplish our goals. The nature and depth of our relationships with others often determine our success in each situation.

Take an analogy from geology. We're all familiar with graphite and diamond. These substances might seem utterly different. Graphite is soft, dull, and opaque, well suited as an industrial lubricant. Diamond is hard, brilliant, and transparent, often used to cut other tough materials. Yet both substances are made entirely of carbon. How can two things with dramatically different characteristics be made of the same thing? In graphite, the carbon atoms are connected in sheets that easily slough off. In diamonds they fit in a tetrahedral pattern that creates some of the strongest bonds in the universe. The kinds of connections make all the difference.

Boris Groysberg of Harvard Business School and colleagues studied "superstar" employees who excelled at one company and then left for another.[2] Most of them struggled to replicate their success. He attributed the difference partly to their lack of relationships. They were still highly capable, but needed several years to rebuild a network of trusted ties to get things done. Most of these superstars were individual performers, not managers of teams. If they struggled without relationships, it's even harder for leaders, who must work through others. Focusing on individual capabilities at the expense of relationships has become a trap.

Recognizing this phenomenon, consultants and academics are changing how they think about leadership. Beginning with the rise of leader-member exchange theory, definitions of leadership have shifted. Instead of defining it by individual behaviors or competencies, experts have come to view it as a dynamic, two-way relationship between a leader and a follower. Marshall Goldsmith, a best-selling author, and his coauthor say flatly, "Leadership, it's clear from this research, is a relationship."[3]

We've long understood that leadership doesn't exist in a vacuum, that you can't have a leader without a follower. But now we're seeing that leaders need a lot of peer support as well. Even the act of leading emerges more from multiple people than from a single heroic individual. Thus the US Army, famous for its hierarchies, is exploring leadership as a group rather than an individual phenomenon. Created in response to the complex, ill-defined problems of asymmetric warfare, the Army developed a framework for "collective leadership."[4] Members of an organization share leadership rather than place it in the hands of a single person. This approach improves adaptability by enabling leadership to flow across the organization's network to the individuals with the most relevant skills and expertise in any given situation.

How we view leadership matters, because it eventually drives how real leaders act. Smart leaders can now get on board and see leadership for what it truly is—a social relationship between individuals. That relationship-based approach better reflects how people and organizations truly work now (see Figure 2.1).

Most leaders still pay too little attention to networks of relationships. When they think about the organization and their place in it, they focus on the formal org chart or maybe a value stream map. Those charts represent a theory of how work gets done, but in the real world, organizations work mainly through networks of relationships. Leaders who tune their network for their specific goals and understand the many ways those relationships can help them are much better equipped to lead in complex times.

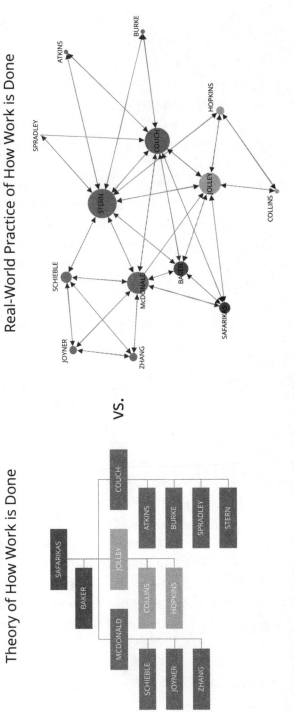

Formal Structure
Theory of How Work is Done

VS.

Informal Network
Real-World Practice of How Work is Done

FIGURE 2.1 Formal structure versus informal network

The Invisible Advantage: Informal Relationships

From our experience working with leaders and studying how they interact with others, we've identified several ways that networks provide a competitive advantage. Networks foster strategic perspective, influence, creativity, collaboration, force multiplication, and well-being.

Leaders who maintain a broad set of relationships, extending not only throughout but also beyond their own organization, improve their *strategic perspective*. They are better able to see the big picture. Their network gives them insight into others' points of view. They can discover emerging threats and opportunities faster, better understand how their organization operates, and pinpoint what matters most.

A network also provides *influence*. It extends a leader's reach. The writer Malcolm Gladwell contrasts the midnight rides of Paul Revere and William Dawes. Both set out on horseback April 18, 1775, to warn people that British troops were coming to seize munitions and arrest resistance leaders. While Revere successfully alerted thousands of colonists, Dawes roused far fewer. Gladwell attributes Revere's effectiveness to his influence: he knew more people in the towns he visited, especially those who were well connected and could best spread the message.[5]

Networks foster *creative ideas*. When we rely on information from just immediate team members, we are susceptible to groupthink. Alternatively, when we're connected with people who think and behave differently, we can combine their knowledge and perspective to create something new. As Steve Jobs said, "Creativity is just connecting things." Sociologist Ron Burt found that managers with more diverse connections—connections to people from separate groups, which are not themselves connected—are more likely to come up with good ideas.[6]

We can see this creativity in the culinary arts. Massimo Bottura owns Osteria Francescana, a Michelin three-star eatery in Modena,

Italy, rated among the world's best restaurants. Although Bottura is also the main chef, he seeks a diversity of perspective in his two sous chefs: Italian Davide di Fabio and Japanese Kondo Takahiko. Di Fabio prefers improvisation, while Takahiko seeks precision. Bottura uses his relationships with both to manage the resulting "collisions," which promote not just innovation but also inspire curiosity in other workers.

Most obviously, our connections facilitate *collaboration*, working with people outside of our immediate team or department. Mike Theilmann was chief human resources officer at Albertsons, the nation's second largest grocery chain, when the COVID-19 pandemic hit. For the first time in a generation, people were shopping at grocery stores more than going out to restaurants. Theilmann and his team suddenly had to hire tens of thousands of employees to meet demand. Albertsons then still relied on older technology platforms to recruit and hire, and didn't even have a career website.

Realizing Albertsons' traditional hiring approach wouldn't work, Theilmann and his team leveraged their connections. Their recruiters reached out to HR executives they knew and established handshake partnerships with 35 companies, many in the travel and hospitality space, that had to furlough employees. "We told them, we'll take care of your people. At some point, you'll want them back and we'll be overstaffed given the peaks we're hitting now. It will be good for them, good for you, and good for us." These relationships with companies such as Marriott and Delta Airlines enabled Albertsons to fill 65,000 roles in three months, kept thousands of people employed, and helped to maintain the nation's food supply in the pandemic.[7]

Relationships work both ways: leaders get ideas and resources, but they can also share ideas and resources with others. By providing others with guidance, coaching, and feedback, leaders can bring out the best in them. A leader's network becomes a *force multiplier*, expanding the capabilities of those with whom the leader works.

Unfortunately, leaders too often shy away from coaching and sharing feedback. We've found that the amount of performance feedback given by leaders varies widely. At one global life science company we studied, some leaders gave 20 times more feedback than others, and 15% of employees received no feedback whatsoever. Besides the irony that these performance management discussions are one of the few conversations mandated by organizations, the paucity of feedback makes it harder for employees, and the organization, to learn and adapt. In the same study we found that employees receiving the most feedback were far more likely to be top performers. When leaders don't share feedback, they miss the opportunity to improve their employees' capabilities and ensure that people work on the right things.

Leaders' relationships don't just provide conduits for feedback; they also foster overall employee engagement. In much of the 20th century, companies could expect to hire recruits who would commit to decades of working steadily up the hierarchy. Leaders took a degree of loyalty and commitment as a given. But the pandemic shattered what was already a weakening bond between employers and employees. As the spread of "quiet quitting" demonstrates, employees are increasingly apt to put in the bare minimum. Absent any special ties, employees focus on their own career goals and give companies only what they expect to earn equivalently in return. Leaders who cultivate relationships have a chance to build trust, win over these employees, and increase their discretionary effort.

Leaders' relationships with employees are likely to matter more as some degree of remote work continues at many companies. A recent study examined thousands of teams in a wide range of jobs. Leadership focused on relationships (participative, empowering) achieved better virtual team performance than task-focused leadership (directive, controlling), particularly in larger teams where it was harder to "see" what colleagues were doing.[8]

Finally, setting aside a leader's business effectiveness, relationships improve their well-being. For decades, scientists have studied how social connections affect our health. They've found that the greater the number and diversity of our ties, the healthier we are. Social networks reduce our vulnerability to cardiovascular disease, cancer, cognitive abilities, even the common cold. Those relationships also boost our mental health, including cognitive abilities, self-esteem, and happiness. Relationships are the foundation of our lives.

It's not just our direct connections who affect us. Researchers Nicholas Christakis and James Fowler examined the impact of networks on individual happiness through three degrees of relationships. The first degree comprises the people you know directly, the second are the people those people know, and the third comprises the people those people know. Christakis and Fowler found that if first-degree people are happy, your likelihood of happiness increases by 20%. If people in the second degree are happy, your chances increase by 15%, and the happiness effect for people in the third degree is still significant at 10%.[9] Amazingly, they saw an influence on your happiness from people you may never meet.

One way that remote influence works is by buffering or insulating us from negative events. Sheldon Cohen, a relationship researcher and psychologist at Carnegie Mellon University, says that "having people who you think will provide you with help when you need it, helps protect you from the effects of stress on your health."[10] Even imagined protection, such as the belief that someone would support you in a difficult situation, can have a real and positive impact on an individual's well-being.

Fluid Networks: A Key to Dynamic Leadership

Leaders have multiple reasons to bolster and expand their relationships, but the central one is to perform better in complex business environments. As in the graphite and diamond analogy, it is the connections between the parts, more than the properties of the parts themselves, that primarily determine what a system can do. And fortunately, unlike those static minerals, dynamic relationships give leaders enormous flexibility. The ability to reconfigure relationships is essential to the success of complex adaptive systems. Similar to a communication network that automatically reroutes traffic in the event of a fault, leaders can draw on their connections to quickly address emerging opportunities and threats. In essence, they can act like graphite when they need to lubricate machine parts and turn into diamond when they need to cut glass.

The ability of a complex adaptive system's multiple, diverse parts to flexibly interact is a powerful capability that many organizations have sought to exploit. John Kotter calls for a *dual operating system*, and Michael Arena calls for *adaptive space*. In both approaches the idea is to create a network of stakeholders from across the enterprise who share ideas and learn from each other. They can collaborate outside the formal chain of command to address new strategic opportunities and threats. Relationships are the infrastructure that enable these forums.

Some companies have gone as far as to largely do away with formal structure. Founded by two ex-Microsoft employees in 1996, Valve, a global leader in video gaming, replaced formal hierarchy entirely with an informal "boss-less" structure in which employees decide for themselves which projects to work on, how to spend their time, and even how much to pay colleagues. The only constraints come in the form of simple rules, such as the rule of three, which states that a project can be started only if at least three employees agree to work on it. That's surprising to those who believe that you need a driving individual with a singular vision to create something truly creative. Yet the firm created *Half Life*, one of the most successful video games ever using their collaborative approach. Even the organization's strategy emerges bottom-up. For example, Steam, the company's highly successful digital video game storefront and distribution service, which represented a strategic pivot for Valve, came from employees without management direction or market research.

Although some have suggested Valve's approach to organizing isn't scalable or fosters a cliquish culture, it's hard to argue with its success. Steam is the mostly widely used video game distribution platform in the world with about 75% market share, and Valve likely has higher revenue per employee than Google, Amazon, or Microsoft.

Whether through stronger informal networks or outright "bossless-ness," leaders are working to dissolve silos and encourage employees to forge relationships across the organization. By equipping employees to share information, solve problems, and collaborate, organizations expand the solutions they bring to bear on emerging problems and perishable opportunities in the market. The dynamic ability of these companies to reconfigure relationships makes them more adaptive to changing environments.

A Path to Strong Networks

Despite the central role of relationships in leading through complexity, many leaders are slow to appreciate their value. This isn't surprising when you consider that early in their careers, as Ivan Berg described, many leaders operated within a single department or assumed specific, functional roles. Influence came mainly from their expertise or their formal authority.

Additionally, few leaders receive training in effective collaboration. In her research, Dr. Bonita Thompson, managing director of The Chief Executive Alliance, found that most executives learn to collaborate through trial and error or early childhood experiences, such as growing up in a large family or playing sports.[11] As a result, leaders may neglect relationships, focusing instead on building up their skills, knowledge, and positional power. Some simply perceive developing their network as a distraction from "real work."

That mindset leaves them unprepared for larger responsibilities and vulnerable to failure. Our research in one technical professional organization suggests that the structure, or pattern, of a leader's network of relationships, better predicts their performance than education, experience, and cognitive abilities combined. Furthermore, as leaders progress, they must manage an increasingly larger set of relationships. The average manager handles 17 relationships, the average director maintains 40, and the average C-level executive 205.[12] Those leaders who don't appreciate their network as they move up often wonder why they're no longer able to make things happen.

Jeff, the chief information officer at a global consumer goods company, won the job in 2019 because of his impressive success at a smaller firm. A year in he was struggling. He led a group of over a thousand people, and his approach seemed sound. He introduced a matrixed operating model to collaborate with the business units, a near-necessity as the company had expanded to over a hundred countries with dozens of brands. He also made a priority of building out the company's e-commerce platform. But now the CEO was looking over his shoulder, questioning his leadership.

It turns out that Jeff saw his role mainly through his own capabilities and decisions, not his relationships with others. He focused on his plan, leaving little time for the people who would make it happen. When he took the job, he brought over several colleagues, and those on the team who hadn't come over with him felt left out. They saw the new people having Jeff's ear, leaving them with little influence.

As a result, those legacy team members pursued their own agenda rather than Jeff's. Moreover, the people he brought with him, sensing the internal division, started to diversify their risk by focusing on furthering their own careers. There was too little trust for the group to work effectively, dissension was rife, and major projects were missing deadlines. On paper everything looked as it should, and Jeff couldn't pinpoint the problem. But the e-commerce platform was stalled, and his career hung in the balance.

The first step to avoiding the trap is simply to recognize our outdated ideas. We fall into the trap because it matches most of what we've learned in life. "When in doubt, our culture leans toward competition over collaboration," points out Tom Bigda-Peyton, the former chief learning officer at Catholic Health. "This can be a good thing when it's a healthy competition. But it can also make it hard to collaborate across disciplines when we face complex, interdependent challenges."[13] The emphasis on competition is built into a lot of our education and advancement. So people have a false belief that success relies solely on individual capabilities.

To dig out of the trap, leaders have to change their frame of reference. Instead of seeing everyone solely as individuals, with their own separate accountabilities, start seeing networks of people accomplishing what individuals can't do well on their own. Once you see the power of networks, you'll have extra motivation to invest in relationships. It's not easy for those of us raised in cultures that emphasize and reward individual excellence. But there's plenty of room for individual initiative within networks.

Even leaders who appreciate the power of networks can stumble by emphasizing task-focused relationships at the expense of social-emotional ties. Task-oriented relationships highlight the objectives, not the people. They tend to be temporary and typically involve setting goals, generating ideas, solving problems, making decisions, or crafting plans related to the task at hand. Socio-emotional relationships, by contrast, center on building and maintaining close personal connections that persist over time. These tend to be less formal and often involve sharing emotional experiences and feelings.

It's understandable that leaders often prioritize task-focused relationships. After all, the purpose of these relationships is to get work done. Yet as we've seen, leaders today must work across organizational silos and even companies. They can no longer count solely on their own expertise or positional power to tell others what to do. Instead, they must leverage the other primary form of influence—socio-emotional relationships. When we have a strong positive relationship with someone, characterized by trust, warmth, and mutual respect, we are more likely to listen carefully and ultimately act on what they say.

In fact, leaders who rely exclusively on task-focused relationships tend to be feared, envied, or even resented by those they work with. These leaders have demonstrated their capability but not their positive intent. The other extreme isn't much better. Some leaders are so worried about being liked that they can't make decisions or act decisively. Leaders need both. In one study, being perceived by others as both competent and warm together accounted for 90% of why people choose to follow someone.[14] As psychologists Rob Kaiser and

Bob Kaplan articulate in their work on leadership versatility, different situations call for different approaches. Leaders whose networks balance task-focused and socio-emotional relationships have a greater breadth of resources to draw on.

Another challenge for leaders is to avoid connecting only with people similar to themselves. This isn't surprising as it's easier to build relationships with others who are like us. Having things in common creates a sense of shared experiences and identity, making us feel comfortable and familiar with one another. This is one reason why we ask people on first meeting them questions such as "Where did you grow up?," "Do you have kids?," and "What do you do for work?" With each question, we're looking for a common experience on which to build a relationship.

In many ways, building strong relationships with and embedding in networks of people who are like us serves us well. It makes us feel safe and promotes interpersonal understanding. In working together, we don't step on each other's toes and things don't fall through the cracks.

The downside is that networks of similar people are more vulnerable to groupthink. They turn into echo chambers and reject new ideas as "not invented here." The lack of diverse thinking makes it hard to come up with innovative ideas, recognize when circumstances change, or challenge the prevailing view. This tendency toward homogeneity in thinking is one reason for the failure of the intelligence community in the lead-up to the second Persian Gulf war.

The bias toward similarity also disadvantages colleagues from non-majority populations. If people are prone to forging relationships with those like themselves, and straight white males dominate the leadership ranks, it will be hard for female leaders, leaders of color, or LBGTQ leaders to build the relationships needed for advancement. This is one important challenge that diversity programs can help to overcome by encouraging the formation of connections across demographic differences. As described by David Thomas, president of Morehouse College, "People of color who advance the furthest all share one characteristic—a strong network of mentors and corporate sponsors who nurture their professional development."[15]

Leaders can overcome this tendency by purposefully building relationships with people different from themselves. Push yourself outside your comfort zone. Actively seek out people with unfamiliar backgrounds or perspectives. Ask yourself what you can learn from them even when you disagree.

Finally, leaders need to resist the idea that more is better. Based on the size of the human brain, Robin Dunbar, an evolutionary psychologist at Oxford University, determined 30 years ago that people can maintain approximately 150 stable relationships.[16] *Dunbar's number*, as it came to be called, comes from the insight that humans have a limited capacity for social interaction as maintaining relationships requires a significant cognitive effort. Relationships are not born out of charisma; they take work. As a result, most people limit the number of close relationships they have in order to avoid cognitive overload. Researchers have confirmed Dunbar's number in a wide variety of settings, from weddings to military units and church parishes.

Note that Dunbar's number refers to the total number of stable relationships we can maintain. That's not the same thing as close, meaningful ties. Dunbar suggested that we can have no more than 15 "best friends." In the same vein, Rob Cross, a professor of global leadership at Babson College, and his coauthor found that effective leaders maintain a core network of just 12–18 people.[17] These are the people for whom you would go out of your way to help and who would do the same for you. With too few of these connections, leaders are likely working without the resources they need. Too many and they risk collaborative overload.

Leaders must decide where to place their bets. If they can maintain only 12 to 18 strong connections, whom should they include? Is it better to have access to creative ideas, organizational influence, or personal support? Would you rather help your nearby colleagues develop their capabilities or establish many relationships that will expose you to different parts of the business? The answers depend on your goals as a leader. What's most important is that you spend time thinking about the best way to optimize your network.

Escaping the Trap

In simpler times, leaders could rely on their formal position in the hierarchy to create the relationships needed to carry out the job. So they could focus on building their own skills and accomplishments, and leverage their formal authority to influence others. But with the imperative of developing a complex adaptive system, ready to respond to opportunities and threats, leaders must look to people beyond their chain of command. They need trusting relationships with a diverse set of colleagues, across the enterprise. Those colleagues will then act as multipliers, extending and amplifying the leader's impact.

Leaders who rely solely on their own expertise and experience, and don't appreciate the value of relationships, risk lacking the resources to face unpredictable challenges. This makes an already tough job impossible. The best leaders recognize that much of the real work in their organization now happens despite the formal organization. They continually assess and tune their informal network based on what they want to achieve and the circumstances at hand.

3

The Vulnerability Paradox

The year was 2010. Commanding General of US Forces in Iraq, Lloyd Austin, and US ambassador to Iraq, James Jeffrey, were in uncharted waters. They sat facing each other in the center of the room, surrounded by senior onlookers, in an undisclosed location in Bagdad. They'd just been asked, "What do you each need to do differently as the leaders of your respective organizations?"

Only weeks before, the two had assumed their respective roles and been charged with leading Operation New Dawn. They had 15 months to transition from a military to a civilian mission. It was the largest transition of a mission in modern US history, and radically different from anything General Austin or Secretary Jeffrey had done before. Getting it right would require extraordinary collaboration between the military and State Department.

Both institutions are effective at top-down, command-and-control operations, but they have different worldviews, so they often work at cross purposes. General Austin and Secretary Jeffrey knew the institutions would need to engage with one another in new ways to pull off the mission in the fraught environment of post-invasion Iraq. The two leaders would have to build a team of teams that spanned both organizations.

Our friend Chris Ernst, currently chief learning officer at Workday, was there that day to facilitate the 16-hour "combined vision development" meeting with the general, ambassador, and senior division commanders, general officers, and counselor-level embassy personnel. Ernst remembers, "We asked both the General and the Ambassador to share what they each had to do differently for the partnership to work. It was a key moment. They had to show real vulnerability. That's not the world that generals and ambassadors live in. They stepped outside their comfort zone, and it set the stage for the tremendous partnership that followed."[1]

The Confidence Trap

Leaders have long been inclined to avoid any show of vulnerability, lest they lose the all-important authority needed to be effective. But researchers have lately found this to be a trap. Vulnerability actually bolsters leaders, in part by encouraging the relationships discussed in Chapter 2. What's more, colleagues are now less likely to look down on vulnerability.

Brené Brown, a best selling author and academic researcher in vulnerability, defines it as "the emotion that we experience during times of uncertainty, risk, and emotional exposure."[2] For Brown, vulnerability is a critical ingredient in any endeavor in which one fully commits themselves. You can't be all-in if you're unwilling to put your defenses aside. As a result, giving and receiving feedback, taking risks, solving problems, and making big decisions all involve making ourselves vulnerable around others.

Indeed, accepting our fallibility is also just part of life, and leaders are better off applying the energy of covering weaknesses to productive areas. We are not our job titles. We are human beings and all of us—including leaders—struggle with anxiety, stress, and other difficulties. In one study, researchers asked 30 leaders from global corporations, national and international charities, and startups to keep a journal for one month and answer prompts, such as "What is emerging for you?" According to the study's authors, every leader experienced major emotional turmoil.[3] It's no wonder that one in five CEOs now seek therapy.[4]

In a broader sense, accepting fallibility has become a reality of corporate life. Corporate longevity continues to decline. Average tenure on the Fortune 500 list has dropped by almost half since the late 1970s.[5] Prior to stepping down as CEO of Cisco Systems in 2015, John Chambers bluntly told attendees at a conference, "40 percent of businesses . . . unfortunately, will not exist in a meaningful way in ten years. If I'm not making you sweat, I should be."[6] Just about every company is susceptible to discontinuities: from global pandemics to geopolitical conflict, climate disasters, political uncertainty, or supply chain disruption. Even Big Tech mainstays such as Amazon and Netflix—seemingly unbeatable a few years ago—are now in tough competition with high-focused upstarts, such as Chewy, and deep-pocketed streaming services.

Vulnerability Is a Catalyst for Adaptation

Ironically, leaders who lean into their fallibility and express vulnerability have an easier time navigating today's disruptive world than those who deny it. First and foremost, expressing vulnerability helps leaders to stay current. When we recognize that our knowledge is finite, what psychologist Tenelle Porter and her coauthors call *intellectual humility*, we're more open to exploration and considering the views of others.[7] Moreover, embracing our fallibility gives leaders a kind of permission with colleagues, and with themselves, to ask the "dumb" questions that often uncover profound information. This is particularly important in rapidly changing situations where time-to-insight is a deciding factor between success or failure.

Also, it's only by acknowledging our fallibility that we're able to recognize our mistakes and grow. If we can't admit when we've done something wrong, it's difficult to adapt. Yet many leaders go down in flames because they resist this move and double down on bad decisions. For these leaders, looking smart is more important than being right. These leaders are prone to what psychologist Carol Dweck calls a *fixed mindset*.[8] They view failure as defining the limit of their capabilities, instead seeing it as an opportunity to learn and grow through self-reflection, hard work, and dialogue.

Expressing vulnerability also helps us manage the elephant in the room. Everyone deals with difficult emotions. When we deny them, they often come back stronger, damaging our behavior, decision-making, and mental health. When we name and acknowledge our emotions, we reduce their power over us and better control how we respond.

A sense of our own fallibility is also what enables us to ask for help. Individuals just can't effectively address complex situations on their own. Too many variables, interacting in too many ways, make it impossible for one person to grasp all potential developments. Leaders need information and wisdom from multiple angles and perspectives in order to chart an effective strategy, and that's possible only through collaboration. When we acknowledge our own limitations, we open space for others to step up.

David Chang, now president and chief technology officer of WuXi AppTec's Advanced Therapies unit, demonstrates this point. Born in Taiwan, he attended college in the United States and went to work in the development function of a large pharma company. After several years in the United States and Switzerland, he became general manager for one of the company's manufacturing sites in Shanghai.

Chang remembers, "When I first showed up there were 800 people in the site's auditorium, clapping and nodding at everything I said." He soon realized that people were expecting him to know everything, when he actually had big gaps. "My experience was in biologics [large molecule], and this was small molecules. I'd been in technical development, and this was operations. I spoke Chinese but I hadn't worked for a Chinese company. People were just going along with whatever I said even if I didn't know what I was talking about."[9]

In desperation, he started saying, "I don't know," when asked to decide. Some of his lieutenants started freaking out. His HR leader even told him, "You might want to tone down the 'I don't knows' or you risk losing people's confidence." But he felt he didn't have a choice. "It's not like it's Silicon Valley. You can't fake it till you make it in that environment. 'I told them, you guys are operations experts.' 'I bring different expertise.'" He started insisting that everyone in his team meetings share their opinion. When most of the team chose one course of action over another, he would back it. "People started to realize their perspective mattered. It changed the culture."

Eventually, Chang's factory became the most productive of all the company's manufacturing sites in the world, and employee engagement skyrocketed. "They ended up calling me back to Switzerland [headquarters] to explain how we'd done it," he remembers. "They'd never seen anything like it before."

When leaders role model vulnerability, they demonstrate that it's okay to not have all the answers, even make mistakes. This helps generate psychological safety on a team. Defined by professor Amy Edmondson as the belief that one can speak up without risk of punishment or humiliation, psychological safety encourages people to surface challenges sooner, boosts creativity, promotes ambitious goals, decreases tension, and creates space for sensitive conversations. Although some leaders worry that sharing their own mistakes will legitimize missteps, the truth is the opposite. In one study, when leaders shared their own mistakes in addressing ethical challenges, employees were less likely to engage in unethical behavior.[10]

When leaders maintain a façade of perfection, they inadvertently encourage the fear of failure. Colleagues hesitate before stepping outside their comfort zone. They cover up mistakes and point the finger at others when things go wrong. As Brown points out, "No vulnerability, no creativity. No tolerance for failure, no innovation. It is that simple. If you're not willing to fail, you can't innovate. If you're not willing to build a vulnerable culture, you can't create."[11]

Vulnerability Breaks Down Barriers

Best of all, being open about your inadequacies draws people in. Professor Jeff Polzer calls this the *vulnerability loop*. When one person shares a failing, it creates space for others to do the same. The exchange becomes a high-candor interaction that builds trust. Vulnerability loops are particularly potent when something has gone wrong or conflict arises. According to Polzer, "At those moments, people either dig in and become defensive, and start justifying, and a lot of tension gets created. Or they say something like, 'Hey, that's interesting. I'm curious and want to talk about it some more.' What happens in that moment helps set the pattern for everything that follows."[12]

That's true even with online meetings. In working with colleagues they've never met in person, leaders may think they need to project a strong image. But researchers have found that virtual teams actually improve their connection and performance by talking about personal struggles. In one study, subjects answered questions such as, "What is an important memory from your childhood that makes you feel sad?" The groups with those questions collaborated better than groups with less personal questions.[13]

Colleagues appreciate a leader for being "real" or "genuine," for not projecting a false front. Moreover, when we try to deceive, it's likely to backfire. Most people excel at reading people's affect, so they can tell someone who is holding back. Paula Niedenthal, a psychologist at the University of Wisconsin-Madison, says, "We are wired to read each other's expressions in a very nuanced way. This process is called 'resonance' and it is so automatic and rapid that it often happens below our awareness."[14]

Just by looking at someone, we experience them. That's why when we see someone stub their toe, we'll often feel our own twinge of pain. Similarly, watching someone smile stimulates our own smile muscles. Ulf Dimberg, a researcher at Uppsala University in Sweden, found that when we suspect a smile is fake, the expression is more likely to make us uncomfortable rather than comfortable.

That resonance happens even if we aren't conscious of it. James Gross, a researcher at Stanford University, found that when someone feels angry but keeps their anger bottled up, people may not consciously recognize the anger, but their own blood pressure goes up nonetheless.[15]

Alternatively, when we're up front about how we're feeling, we deepen our relationships by building trust. That can feel risky—what if your colleague loses respect for you or you jeopardize the authority of your position? But what is trust for, if not to take risks? As we saw in the last chapter, trustful relationships are critical to our ability to thrive in complex environments.

Why Leaders See Vulnerability as a Showstopper

Despite these benefits, vulnerability remains a nonstarter for many executives. They've learned the opposite lesson as they climbed the corporate hierarchy. In order to win promotions, they had to demonstrate not just excellence at their level but a readiness to move to the next level. They also had to outmaneuver colleagues who wanted the same step up, so they kept any exposed weaknesses to a minimum. Showing vulnerability amounted to taking yourself out of the game.

Here they can learn from Neil, who seemed the epitome of a successful leader. He began his career with an established global retail company. After a few promotions there and success at an e-commerce startup, he landed the big job as the CEO of a much larger online retailer.

Neil knew he'd have to work on winning over his executive team, most of whom had been together since the company's early years. His outsider status and his largely corporate experience were likely to rub them the wrong way.

So he doubled down on an approach that had worked in the past. He confidently asserted his views about how to address the company's many challenges. The board had hired him to go global and expand the company's offerings. They wanted results fast, so he knew he needed to move quickly.

Unfortunately, that confidence backfired, alienating his new colleagues. They were already suspicious of him, and his know-it-all approach only confirmed their fears. Because he had the full backing of the board, they couldn't object directly. They responded by checking out. If he was so confident, what did he need them for anyway?

Neil was so concerned about seeming credible that he didn't notice their withdrawal. He readily got the floor at meetings, but his ideas never seemed to gain traction. He was so busy demonstrating his expertise that he didn't solicit his colleagues' perspectives, and they weren't eager to volunteer.

Neil had fallen into the common trap of presenting himself as the capable leader fully in command of the situation. This approach was viable in previous decades, when industries and competition were fairly stable and boundaries clear. Leaders could figure out the "right" answer and then rely on their positional power to get others to execute. The main leadership challenge was to establish authority; once you achieved this, you could expect follow-through. So you spent a lot of time jockeying for position and then figuring out the strategy. Your influence came from your position, and the hierarchy drove most of the real activity in the firm.

That very influence paradoxically makes leaders fearful, lest they not fit the part. One study of more than 100 CEOs and other executives found they most feared being found incompetent. Other top fears included underachieving, appearing vulnerable or foolish, and being politically attacked by colleagues. Together these fears resulted in leaders' inability to have honest conversations. Instead, they played politics, disowned problems, and tolerated bad behaviors.[16]

Their fears are understandable. After all, leaders feel constant pressure to perform at a high level. We expect them to have the right vision, bring it to fruition, and answer tough questions along the way. That encourages arrogance. They tell themselves, "If I'm the one making all the tough decisions and working harder than everyone else, then why shouldn't everybody just listen to me?"

Robert Iger, in his initial retirement as Disney CEO in 2020, told an interviewer, "I became a little bit more dismissive of other people's opinions than I should have been. It wasn't the reason I left, but it was a contributing factor." He was saying no too often to his colleagues, because he had "heard every argument before."[17]

When you're the boss with large swaths of people reporting to you, it's easy to get caught up. Your very identity comes from people looking to you for answers. Your path to success means you're likely good at what you do with few failures. As the late Chris Argyris famously explained, this identity as a highly successful professional makes it hard to learn.[18] When your sense of self-worth is based on your perceived intelligence and track record of success, it is all too easy to stray from self-confidence into intellectual arrogance and discount or dismiss challenging information. When you don't understand something, you assume it's irrelevant. When people share challenging feedback, you ignore it, get defensive, or blame others. Like a sophisticated ostrich, you keep your head in the sand.

Leaders can escape this loop if they focus on what their teams need to be effective. Early in his career, one of us (Dan) evaluated Jim, a successful stock trader who had been outfitted with an executive coach by his global investment bank. Dan had rarely seen such low scores on collegiality and interpersonal sensitivity, and gently told him so. Jim wasn't fazed at all; he introduced Dan to some of his colleagues on the trading floor, and Dan soon realized that the trader's approach was likely the norm for his environment and frankly a reasonable survival mechanism.

When Dan asked whom he admired most, Jim quickly noted his boss, Frank. He described him as "not an a-hole" and a person you can trust, someone who is genuinely interested in the team being successful. He expressed admiration for Frank's willingness to express self-doubt and anxiety about trades. Frank didn't worry about people using his vulnerability against him, and Jim admired and respected him for it. Dan asked Jim why he didn't try to be more like Frank, and they agreed that this would be a worthy goal for his coaching.

Some leaders shy away from vulnerability for fear of the impact it will have on the team. As author Simon Sinek points out, "When you occupy a position of leadership, a whisper becomes a shout; everything is amplified."[19] Lower-level employees can express uncertainty or doubt about the company's prospects, but leaders don't have the same luxury. If a leader publicly expresses concerns, they risk demoralizing others. Fearing this outcome, many leaders choose to keep their concerns to themselves.

In addition, many organizations do not provide a format or setting for dialogue that encourages vulnerability. Most meetings between employees are either operational, focusing on what to do and how to do it, or social, focusing on team building and having fun. This "work-hard, play-hard" dichotomy leaves little room for discussing feelings. Although one-on-one performance and development conversations give employees a chance to talk about their experiences and aspirations, these discussions are often tied to evaluations and compensation. As a result, employees may be reluctant to share their true feelings. They aren't vulnerable, so their managers aren't either.

Demonstrating vulnerability can be even more difficult for leaders from disadvantaged populations, such as women and people of color. These leaders are still underrepresented in many companies. Because they don't look like others in their organizations, they often believe they have to compensate by being better, smarter, stronger. These leaders may also feel pressure to succeed as the sole representative of their population. And because they are not in the majority group, they bear greater risk of reprisals when they speak up or buck the status quo. All leaders take risks in veering from norms, but these leaders risk the most. Social and personality psychologist Chelsea Mitamura nonetheless makes the point that "in an increasingly diverse workforce, these leaders have a unique opportunity to role model vulnerability and show its value to those who do not often see themselves reflected in leadership."[20]

Indeed, it's the very difficulty of showing vulnerability that makes it work. The act of admitting shortcomings or failures often surprises employees. The surprise pulls them into the moment. It focuses their attention and generates curiosity. They have to think harder and make sense of what the leader is doing.

Cultivating Vulnerability

How can leaders check their arrogance? How can they share their vulnerability without undermining their credibility?

One way is for leaders to be honest about the difficulties they face. According to Leena Nair, chief human resources officer at Unilever, "The most effective way for leaders to bring a sense of purpose, service, compassion, and empathy into the workplace is to be transparent about the challenges in their own lives."[21] Brad Smith, CEO of Intuit, exemplified this approach when he shared the results of his 360-feedback assessment with the entire organization.[22] Doing so made him more relatable, opened up space for others to contribute, and started a vulnerability loop.

Sharing challenges doesn't mean telling everyone about your darkest moments. Leaders still need healthy boundaries. For example, a leader with healthy boundaries might acknowledge that they are having a tough day due to personal issues, whereas a leader without boundaries might go into unnecessary detail about their private life. A helpful guideline for maintaining a culture of openness while also setting appropriate boundaries is to consider whether sharing a particular piece of information or engaging in a specific behavior would create undue emotional labor for others. If the answer is yes, it may be wise to hold back and revise your statement or action to avoid oversharing.

Regulating one's emotions is also key to avoiding oversharing or demoralizing colleagues. According to researchers Emma Seppala and Christina Bradley, leaders typically fall into one of three groups in expressing feelings about hardships.[23] The first group emphasizes the positive despite their difficulties. In a crisis, they use their optimism and force of will to reassure others that the organization will prevail no matter what. The second group focuses on devising pragmatic solutions to whatever challenge is causing the turmoil. In both cases, these leaders adopt a brave face and avoid talking about feelings. This emotional suppression often leads to diminished social support, fewer close relationships, and negative emotions as well as health consequences including greater stress, poorer memory, and elevated blood pressure.

The third group acknowledges their fears, anxiety, and other negative feelings. Leaders in this category, however, don't simply blurt out how they're feeling. Instead, they regulate their emotions by pausing to reflect on and reassess the situation before communicating. For example, a leader whose team just lost an important sale might refrain from expressing her initial emotional reaction, which could further demoralize the team. Instead, she might start by reminding herself of "all the wins we've had up until that point," "that the year is not over and there are other opportunities to hit our target," or "that the loss generated valuable insight about what we can do better next time." Having assessed the situation more broadly, the leader might acknowledge her frustration or disappointment to the team but go on to emphasize her confidence in them and how they might handle the next opportunity differently.

In a study during the COVID pandemic, leaders who shared versus suppressed their emotions were more likely to build cohesive, resilient, high-performing teams.[24] By expressing their negative emotions, they lessened the impact of their feelings, increased the empathy between themselves and their employees, and helped employees reframe and overcome their own challenges, ultimately improving enterprise morale and performance.

Being vulnerable isn't just about communicating your challenges or negative emotions. Leaders can also demonstrate vulnerability by stepping outside their comfort zone. Although different leaders struggle with different things (e.g., trusting others more than feels natural, speaking truth to power, or breaking with the status quo), one action that makes many leaders feel particularly vulnerable is apologizing.

Many leaders view saying sorry as akin to admitting weakness, and they fear it will undermine their credibility. They aren't wrong to think this. Psychologists point out that apologizing "rearranges the status hierarchy and makes us beholden, at least temporarily, to the other party."[25] As a result, leaders often avoid or put off an apology. But not apologizing doesn't make the mistake disappear. It only communicates that being "right" is more important than doing what's right.

When leaders do apologize well, they validate the harm caused to others and demonstrate that they are open to doing things differently. A genuine apology can thereby strengthen relationships. And apologies may cost less than leaders think—and even increase a colleague's respect. One study of a program that encouraged doctors to apologize for medical errors found that after the program began, lawsuits dropped 65%.[26]

Another way to show vulnerability is with constructive feedback. Although we typically see those receiving feedback as the vulnerable party, communicating the feedback is also a vulnerable act. It risks damaging a relationship that the leader relies on. As a vice president at a large technology company told us, "I know I need to say something, but I can't afford to upset him. I'm better off having someone who is not great than having someone who is completely checked out."

Avoiding the topic may make things easier in the short run, but it's seldom a good long-term solution. In the absence of information on their performance, employees are likely to take away the message "I'm doing fine" or "My manager doesn't trust me enough to share feedback."

Leaders can also show vulnerability by asking others for help. The request itself communicates imperfection, and it puts the leader at risk of rejection. One leader we know named Jasper was a partner at a management consulting firm. He had spent six months building his firm's first digital application. With the beta product complete, he and his small product team arranged their first pitch meeting.

Miraculously, the Fortune 50 client agreed to use the application to support their enterprise-wide finance transformation. The product team worked diligently to finish the app, collect the client data, and conduct the analysis. But when they went to distribute the individual reports to 500 members of the client's finance organization, something went wrong. No one on the client side could access the reports.

"It was a stupid browser compatibility issue, but we missed the deadline," Jasper remembered. "Our client sponsor was furious. She'd gone out on a limb trying something new and now had 500 employees asking for their promised reports. Meanwhile my fellow partners were screaming, 'What are you guys doing over there? You're risking our relationship with this client over something that's not even core to our business.'"

Jasper assembled the product team in a conference room. "Psychologically, I was devastated. I was suddenly massively aware how different building products is from consulting. In consulting you can work all night to fix the PowerPoint presentation, but it doesn't work that way when you're building a product. I just had to admit to the team that we were in over our heads, and I had no idea how to handle it.

"Everyone looked dejected, and then our lead engineer said, 'We could generate all the reports manually.' I said, 'No way, that will take a week.' Then someone else said, 'What if we asked other people in the firm to help?'"

"That's what we did. We put out the call for help and got 20 people to show up on Superbowl Sunday. We gave them instructions and they built and sent the reports. It wasn't what we originally promised, but it worked. It actually deepened the relationship with the client because they saw we were willing to do what it takes. It became a milestone for our firm. We talk about how we all came together when it mattered most."

A further way to demonstrate vulnerability is with new language. Recall how David Chang encouraged colleagues to speak up by simply saying, "I don't know." When it's important for leaders to share their opinion, they can still encourage dialogue by asking, "Tell me what's wrong with this approach," or "Who has a better idea?"

Finally, leaders can reframe how they think about vulnerability itself. When we ask leaders to identify the opposite of vulnerability, they often answer "strength" or "security." This way of thinking makes it hard to be vulnerable. It suggests that to be vulnerable you need to give up being strong and secure. Who would choose to do that?

Instead, leaders can see vulnerability as the most sustainable path to strength and security. All leaders are fallible, particularly in today's rapidly changing, disruptive world. Admitting that is just being honest. Paradoxically, it's when we try to deny our limitations that we're most fallible. Better to put your uncertainty and insecurity to work for you by sharing your challenges, asking for help, and stepping out of your comfort zone.

Escaping the Trap

As we repeat throughout the book, leaders need to step away from their traditional heroic stance. In the past, their relationships came from their position in the hierarchy. It made sense for them to project an image of strength, control, and certainty to inspire confidence and reinforce the power dynamic between them and their followers. A leader's strength justified that they were the right person for the job.

However, the truth is, we're all fallible. That's truer today when market dynamics can change overnight than ever before. Insisting on strength at the expense of vulnerability has become a trap. All the confidence in the world won't save a leader who implicitly tells colleagues to rely on the top. Leaders unwilling to express uncertainty or doubt or admit mistakes are not just ignoring reality; they're also locking themselves, and their organizations, into decisions that may prove unwise.

Leaders can still project confidence overall, but that confidence must come from the efforts of the full organization, not the person in charge—confidence in Us, not Me. Any one person is fallible, but together we can succeed. Not through hierarchy but collaboration: leaders need to give others the space to raise issues and try out ideas. They can start by expressing their own vulnerability. Doing so not only demonstrates authenticity and builds trust but also invites colleagues to join in overcoming challenges with their own special talents.

4 Stop Strategizing and Start Doing

The United States Golf Association (USGA) is 127 years old, serves 25 million members, and is a far-sighted organization. But sometimes even the best-laid plans aren't enough. In 2020, as the organization prepared to roll out a new three-year strategic plan, the COVID-19 pandemic hit, turning the sports world on its head. Uncertain of what to do, the association leaned into one of its core capabilities: running large championship tournaments.

A typical US Open brings together 200,000 people over the course of a week. Steve Schloss, then chief people officer, pointed out that "running a national event at scale requires you to continually reset goals and targets because every day, every hour even, brings new issues and challenges. You have to be able to pivot in the moment."[1]

In confronting the pandemic, the nonprofit took the same approach, Schloss said. "We asked everyone to put aside what they said they would do in 2020. Instead, we created a new system where each team worked in 7-, 30-, or 90-day sprints. The approach gave people greater control in an environment that felt out of control, with the freedom and tools to constantly assess and reassert what is achievable. It's an approach we'll take forward. We're constantly responding to change and asking everyone in the organization to do the same thing."

By continually adjusting their approach, the USGA successfully navigated the pandemic. It was a significant shift from relying on long-term strategic planning. But it avoided the trap of spending time on priorities, only to find these were no longer relevant because circumstances have changed.

The Lure of Strategy

Strategic thinking took off in the 1960s, during the conglomerate boom, when big companies had a variety of businesses and needed to decide how much to invest in each. It made sense to develop a long-term plan for each business, assess the potential returns, and invest accordingly. And with acquisitions having become a realistic path to quickly gain capabilities or market share, strategists had more options than before.

The Boston Consulting Group (BCG) rode this strategy wave to become a major global firm, while other consultancies also expanded. The goal was to help executives figure out how to maximize their opportunities and gains. The actual execution could be left to middle managers who would carry out plans that cascaded down from headquarters.

Interest in strategy continued into the 1990s despite the decline of conglomerates. Even focused companies, the thinking went, needed to have detailed plans for investment according to a theory of success in their markets. Those blueprints generated priorities, milestones, and metrics to hold people accountable for success.

Strategic planning offers several benefits for companies in stable environments. It clarifies leaders' thinking by investigating and validating their assumptions and logic about the business. It generates a single, forward-looking vision on which the organization and its stakeholders can align. Often, the gap between the organization's current state and the vision motivates and energizes people for change. Strategic planning also guides the allocation of resources and investments, sets priorities, and creates a structure for tracking progress. The work ensures that the business harmonizes with market expectations, is competitively differentiated, makes rational decisions backed by analysis, and focuses its efforts on specific goals.

Strategic planning also feeds the egos of executives. The process assumes that strategizing is the realm of senior leaders—only those at the "top" are far-sighted and smart enough to see into the future and chart a clever path to market dominance. Execution is for lesser mortals down in the hierarchy, who simply carry out instructions.

Strategizing lost some sway with the implosion of the dot-com bubble in 2000. Former Allied-Signal CEO Larry Bossidy had a surprise 2002 bestseller with his *Execution: The Discipline of Getting Things Done*. The strong interest was an early sign that in times of rapid change, execution gets harder and top-down strategizing loses effectiveness. Bossidy argued that companies needed greater connections among strategists, managers, and operators. Consulting firms came around as well, as even BCG began to emphasize implementation of strategies and "enabling" teams to make decisions on their own.

But as disruption has accelerated in our now volatile and uncertain world, up-front centralized strategic planning continues at many companies. Most organizations follow a common process. At the start of the year, planning departments analyze market data and internal core competencies. Leaders hold offsite meetings to discuss the analyses, align on strategic priorities, and identify goals for each operating unit and department. They then cascade these goals down to the middle managers who carry them out in their respective silos. At the end of year, leaders assess results and reward for performance, centered on how well those below executed the strategy.

It's a wonderfully clear, rational, and controlled process, reassuringly top-down for leaders convinced they know what's best. It's also comforting for leaders who fear they don't.

Your Strategic Plan Is Already Obsolete

That process worked well enough for decades, but it has become a trap. Close to two-thirds of large-company CEOs now say their organizations struggle to execute strategy.[2] The problem is so well established that academics have given it two names: strategic dissonance or the strategy/execution gap. The trap stems from several issues.

The first is that complex environments don't stand still while organizations perfect their plans. By the time middle managers get the stone tablets from up high, their front line might look very different from what leaders initially assumed. It gets worse. Not only do environments change rapidly but leaders also have a harder time linking cause and effect or forecasting outcomes. Actions or changes in one part of the business environment can cascade to other places in large and unexpected ways. Events depend more on faraway effects than we know, and the world is less structured and regulated than we assume. So it's hard to trace the cause of a particular outcome or determine which actions will lead to value creation.

With increasing connectivity, we're likely to see more unexpected disruptions, not just pandemics but also political unrest, climate change, wars, and emerging technologies such as artificial intelligence. As the statistician Nassim Nicholas Taleb, author of *The Black Swan*, points out, proliferating global networks, both physical and virtual, inevitably add risks to interdependent systems: pathogens, computer viruses, hacking, terrorism, reckless fiscal or monetary management by institutions or governments, or spectacular acts of terror. Such events, Taleb says, "can create a rolling, widening collapse—a true black swan—in the same way that the failure of a single transformer can collapse an electricity grid."[3]

As events become more emergent and less predictable, up-front strategizing loses its efficacy; historical data is simply less relevant. And because executives are far removed from the emerging reality, they often rely on outdated information. Strategic decisions must be made in real time by teams on front lines. Often, those people are the only ones close enough to see what's actually happening and respond accordingly.

In addition, traditional approaches to cascading strategy don't provide the context needed by those lower down in the hierarchy.

In one organization we studied, the number of employees who fully understood the company's strategy dropped 25% for each level between them and the C-suite. In another study, half of middle managers could not identify one of their company's top five strategic priorities.[4] As in the amusing game of "telephone," in which participants repeat a phrase to neighbors and ultimately garble the message, cascading strategy distorts meaning at each level in the hierarchy, making it harder for employees to understand the strategy's intent or align their actions and decisions. People can't execute a strategy they fail to grasp. This explains why most executives say the biggest challenge to strategy execution is people failing to work together to create change.[5]

Without an understanding of the strategy's broader context, people are likely to miss the big picture. They're simply too focused on the goals handed down to them to see new opportunities to the right or left. Their singular attention on their own strategic goals makes them less likely to collaborate, even though goals increasingly require the integration of diverse expertise from across the enterprise. A mismatch exists between how we cascade strategy (vertically within departments) and how we create value (horizontally, across organizational units). This incongruity further undermines our ability to accomplish the strategy we so carefully craft and communicate.

Top-down strategy also inhibits feedback. Although organizations have several methods for cascading strategy (town halls, departmental and individual goal setting), they do little to encourage communication in the other direction. Even the quaint suggestion box, now the ubiquitous employee engagement survey, rarely results in timely action, which is why a third of surveyed employees find it useless.[6]

When employees do share feedback that questions or contradicts the organization's existing strategy, leaders are quick to label the feedback "resistance to change" rather than respond on its merits. Critical insights, from the very people needed to bring the strategy to life, become an obstacle to be overcome rather than an opportunity to learn from and improve the strategy's effectiveness. This not only undermines the firm's ability to execute but also saps employee engagement as employees are left feeling that their opinions are not valued.

Strategic Doing

For all these reasons, up-front strategic planning is far less effective than it used to be. Instead, companies need to hedge their bets, keep options open, and prepare to pivot on short notice. "Forget three-year plans," one observer advised. "Long-term is a year. Short-term is a month."[7]

The management thinker Henry Mintzberg recognized this declining effectiveness back in 1994. In *The Rise and Fall of Strategic Planning*, he distinguished between deliberate and emergent strategy. Deliberate strategies come from a conscious and systematic process, and emergent strategies arise from the organization's interactions with its environment. The latter are not intentionally created plans, but rather patterns of actions and decisions that emerge as the organization adapts to changing circumstances. Already in the 1990s, Mintzberg saw that managers overestimated their ability to predict the future and to plan for it in a precise and technocratic way. Boxer Mike Tyson made the same point when he famously said, "Everyone has a plan until they get punched in the face."[8]

In a world of continual change, leaders need to shorten the time between when they plan and when they collect feedback on what's working and what's not. Otherwise, they and their organizations risk spending time and resources on outdated goals. Instead of up-front planning followed by a long period of doing, leaders need to continually sense and respond so they can pivot in real time.

Leaders do this by integrating strategy and execution—traditionally, two separate and sequential processes—into a single, unified "strategic doing" approach. Strategic doing differs from strategic planning in three ways. It treats a strategy as a hypothesis, often in the form of an action-result combination—if we take this action, we anticipate achieving this result. The organization then assesses the strategy through experimentation, in a process similar to Agile software development. Rapid test-and-learn cycles show the correctness of the hypothesis and how to improve it. They answer the questions, "Did we achieve the results we expected? Why or why not? And, how should we modify our strategy going forward?" Strategy isn't immutable but continually refined based on interaction with the environment.

Strategic doing also operates on a different time frame—not one to five years ahead, but quarters, months, or even weeks. These short iterations allow for much greater certainty, so planning is more feasible and meaningful.

Execution is likewise quite different under strategic doing. In conventional planning, execution means adhering to a centralized strategic plan, and success depends on how well the plan is carried out. Was the work done on time, in budget, and to the requisite quality standard? In strategic doing, execution means distributed initiative taking, experimenting to see what works, and learning from feedback. Nearly all successful startups, which rely on strategic doing almost by necessity, say that the strategies that worked diverged a great deal from what they originally planned.[9]

Some have expressed concern that strategic doing makes it hard to develop competitive advantage. They say it becomes an excuse for easy-to-reach goals and incremental steps, until rivals get ahead, and the company then moves fast to follow. Strategic doing, however, doesn't eliminate long-term goals. Leaders still need to define the organization's purpose and direction or, as former business school dean Roger Martin puts it, "Where to play and how to win."[10]

In strategic doing, companies simply translate those goals into near-term outcomes, hypothesize about how to achieve them, take action, assess if they've "moved the needle," and finally amplify what works and dampen what doesn't. As described by Remo Ruffini, who turned around the fashion brand Moncler, "You cannot make a three-year plan like 10 years ago. We make a three-year plan, but you have to surf inside this plan because everything changes every day."[11]

Where strategic planning is like writing a script and handing it off to actors to perform, strategic doing is like improvisation. The artists start with a common goal and rules and then perform based on ongoing interaction with themselves and feedback from the audience. Strategic doing doesn't predict the future and act on that prediction. It creates a state of organizational readiness, in which people are aware of the shifting environment and quick to pivot as needed.

Getting Comfortable with Discomfort

To create a culture of strategic doing, leaders first need to get comfortable with being uncomfortable. Roger Martin maintains that executives often fear strategy because it requires them to grapple with an uncertain future and make difficult decisions that limit options. This fear is further amplified by the potential for career-ending mistakes.[12] To alleviate the fear, some executives revert to familiar tactics, approaches, and assumptions. But doubling down on what you already know constrains your options, and often what worked in the past doesn't work in the present.

One way to push beyond traditional ways of thinking is to imagine how different uncertainties might intersect to affect outcomes. Futurists do this first by identifying uncertainties (such as the availability of skilled labor) likely to have an impact. They express each uncertainty as an axis bookended by two opposing scenarios. In the case of labor, the opposing scenarios might be "skilled labor is scarce" and "skilled labor is plentiful." Then futurists cross, or layer, two different uncertainties to create a two-by-two matrix where each quadrant represents a different potential future (see Figure 4.1). The intersection of each set of uncertainties creates myriad potential scenarios for leaders to consider.

By broadening the range of potential futures, leaders stay open to possibilities. When Blockbuster declined to acquire Netflix in late 2000, it was stuck in 20th-century thinking. All it saw was a shaky online business and the recent e-commerce bust. Its leaders couldn't imagine the web's commercial and technological possibilities, and they were isolated from colleagues on the ground who could. They

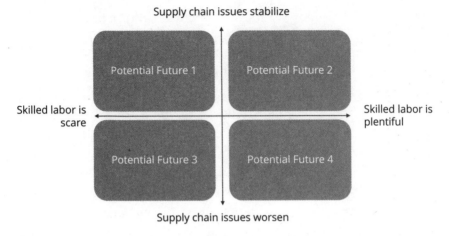

FIGURE 4.1 A sample uncertainty matrix

assumed they could easily imitate Netflix's service and marry it effectively to the profitable brick-and-mortar business. In fact they tried to do that, but organizational pressures forced them to base the online service on the physical stores, which negated much of the potential. Today's organizations that dismiss the impact of generative AI, risk the same fate as Blockbuster.

Top-down strategy can fail even when the leaders' vision is correct. In the mid-1990s, General Motors leaders looked in the future and decided to explore electric vehicles. Because of the company's heavy investment in combustion engines, however, the executives played it safe and created a small, separate division to make the EV-1. Framed as an ongoing engineering experiment, the company only leased the cars, and in just a few cities. Such a narrow roll-out failed to win much enthusiasm, and the company ended the leases after only five years when the regulatory pressure eased.

Soon thereafter, Tesla emerged with a pure-EV strategy, one that it pursued relentlessly, yet with pivots as technology improved and consumer tastes emerged. By 2019, Tesla's market value exceeded GM's. If Blockbuster and GM had imagined a wider variety of potential future outcomes, perhaps they would have made different decisions.

In addition to thinking broadly about potential futures, leaders must keep pace with changes in their environment. An interesting analogy comes from the field of information theory. Mathematician and engineer Claude Shannon was focused on understanding the limits of communications systems at Bell Labs in 1948 when he formulated Shannon's Law, also known as the Nyquist-Shannon Sampling Theorem. It states that to maintain the fidelity of a communication signal, the signal must be sampled at least twice as frequently as the signal changes. Any less and the signal can't be accurately reconstructed. Similarly, the more volatility in the market, the more frequently leaders need to check for changes. If, as in annual strategic planning, leaders sample markets only once a year, they're likely to miss important changes. Applying Shannon's law, if the market is shifting every quarter, leaders need to reexamine their strategy at least every six weeks.

Leaders also need to get comfortable relinquishing some authority. Strategic planning has long made leaders feel smart and in charge. Strategic doing blows this up. Leaders are limited to setting desired outcomes, identifying indicators to track progress, and creating conditions for testing and refining plans. Leaders provide direction without dictating the approach. Although this maximizes the experiences and insights of the organization, leaders need the humility to give up some control.

One approach, embraced by Toyota's leaders, is to make many corporate goals purposely vague so employees can channel their energies in different directions. The goals are still broad enough to force specialists from different functions to collaborate across the rigid silos in which they usually work. Recent goals included reducing tailpipe emissions, preventing accidents, and boosting fuel efficiency. As Zenji Yasuda, a former Toyota executive, points out, if the goals were "more concrete, employees won't be able to exercise their full potential." Vagueness frees "researchers to open new avenues of exploration, procurement to look for new and unknown suppliers who possess needed technology, and sales to consider the next steps needed to sell such products."[13]

Unfortunately, leaders must prepare themselves and their colleagues to be wrong—a lot. That means admitting setbacks (which depend on clear objectives and measurement) and planning for them.

Caterpillar, for example, emerged from the 2008 downturn in relatively good shape—a real success in such a highly cyclical, asset-intensive industry. CEO Douglas Oberhelman credited the company's insistence that each manager take time during strong sales to imagine and think through how they would survive a worst-case scenario. The practice emerged from Oberhelman's experience in Argentina, where sales crashed from 1,200 annual units in the late 1970s to a combined total of four from 1981 to 1983. Under his leadership, the company resisted the temptation to expand aggressively in the booming early 2000s. Caterpillar was less profitable than rivals in those years, but when the recession hit, its balance sheet stayed solid.

Two-Way Transparency

Strategic doing also requires that leaders transparently share information. For the sake of efficiency and their own egos, leaders tend to limit meetings and other interactions with employees sharing only summarized information. The summaries inevitably center on what leaders find important, not what might be useful for the front lines.

Giving employees raw data frees them to draw their own conclusions and insights, rather than limiting them to others' interpretations. They can conduct their own analysis and research, which can lead to creative and effective solutions. Providing raw data also promotes transparency and trust.

That's the method General Stanley McChrystal used when he headed the US joint military force fighting attacks in Iraq. Seeking to break down silos and give everyone the full picture, McChrystal expanded the Joint Special Operations Command's (JSOC) daily huddles from 50 to 7,500 people. The meetings brought together members of the various JSOC teams, including operators, intelligence analysts, and support personnel, to share information and coordinate efforts so they could respond to emerging situations quickly.

Information sharing can't just be top-down, however. It also needs to be bottom up. In its early days, computer animation studio Pixar broke with tradition and started showing daily animation work to the entire special effects crew. Disney animators, by contrast, shared dailies only with a small senior group. Pixar's approach spurred creativity across the group, eliminated surprises, and inspired everyone to raise their game. According to Ed Catmull, cofounder of Pixar, "People's overwhelming desire to make sure their work is 'good' before they show it to others increases the possibility that their finished version won't be what the director wants. The dailies process avoids such wasted efforts," because it forces people to share early.[14]

In *Open Strategy*, professor Christian Stadler and coauthors take bottom-up communication a step further. They advocate for the C-suite to open strategic decision-making to frontline employees, customers, partners, and even rivals. Instead of restricting strategic planning to headquarters, leaders and managers can generate ideas, formulate plans, and implement them in a collaborative way.

We applaud this work, but note that open strategy still separates the strategizing from the implementing. Given the volatility of markets, it's essential that strategies adjust in real time. Hence the Agile metaphor: just as software developers adjust on the fly in response to market signals and internal stresses, strategizers need to modify their plans as conditions change.

Leaders are often reluctant to share information and open the strategy process, and not just for ego reasons—they worry about slowing down their work in order to deal with all sorts of extraneous ideas. But the point is not about delivering a definitive strategy for the company. It's to engage and coordinate the broad organization in meeting emerging threats and opportunities. In many cases, you need to go slow to go fast. Genuine interaction improves outcomes and builds understanding and commitment.

Test, Learn, Strategize

Leaders must do more than simply share information and listen. They need to encourage experimentation. In disruptive environments where you can't discern cause and effect, the only way to figure out what truly works is to try it. Experiments are the mechanism to do that.

Organizations have long used experiments for various applications, from clinical trials and new product features to direct marketing and product development. Companies now need to step up this work. Some organizations have purposely built a capability in this area, such as eBay's Experimentation Platform. Mark Zuckerberg has said he is most proud of his company's framework for relentless testing. "At any given point in time, there isn't just one version of Facebook running, there are probably 10,000. Any engineer at the company can basically decide that they want to test something."[15]

Strategy emerges from these experiments just as much as it directs them. You can collect the wisest, best-informed strategic planning staffers in the world, and you and they are still going to be limited to what you together can foresee. Rather than annual strategizing over a month or two, you'll see farther by evolving your strategy while monitoring ongoing developments and experiments. Jeff Bezos said that Amazon's success "is a function of how many experiments we do per year, per month, per week, per day."[16]

Amazon goes a step further with its $2 > 0$ principle. In the company's early days in the 1990s, Bezos was in a meeting with other executives heatedly debating which of two ideas to pursue. After a while, Bezos quietly went up to the whiteboard, wrote "$2 > 0$," and sat down. His message was clear. In a disruptive environment, speed matters more than efficiency. It's better to test both plausible ideas, as minimum viable offerings at low cost, rather than spend time deliberating on which is better. The executives were arguing largely from ignorance, when real-world testing would settle the question in short order. For projecting into the future, evidence from the real world trumps whatever brilliant plan an executive can concoct.

To sustain experiments, leaders may need to protect colleagues from above. Some companies, such as Amazon until 2021, have dominant owners committed to strategic doing, but others may struggle. Short-sighted investors may try to dictate strategy or micromanage improvements, undermining the flexibility needed for success.

At one company, the CEO saw a major part of his job as "running interference" between the owners and his colleagues. The CEO worked to give his colleagues autonomy in moving the needle on those improvements in response to ongoing market conditions. He "painted the picture" for the owners so his team could carry out the owners' intent.

Here the issue was less about combining strategy and execution, and more about preventing the strategy from becoming so detailed that it hamstrung the managers carrying it out. With the owners, the CEO negotiated general goals, and then worked to maintain flexibility while ensuring accountability and frequent reporting on key numbers. After all, leaders can still develop general goals or paths, in consultation with boards or other parties, but then flesh out those goals in a collaborative, ongoing process with managers and employees on the front lines.

Applying Feedback to Compound Learning

Of course, for experiments to be useful they must provide feedback. We need to know if the experiment worked and why or why not. This means establishing measures, or indicators, that we can examine to see if we're on the right track and what we might want to do differently.

Famously used by Google and now all over Silicon Valley, objectives and key results (OKRs) are one framework for this purpose. In our experience, OKRs work better than other goal setting and measurement approaches, for three reasons. First, they expressly link objectives and key results. Second, they don't predefine the strategy to achieve the objectives. Because circumstances are reliably dynamic, OKRs allow flexibility in the path to accomplish the objective.

Finally, OKRs emphasize the measurement of ongoing progress versus end results. The indicators used in OKRs involve continuous variables, not those with a simple yes or no result. Teams can assess whether they are progressing toward their objective. The conversation becomes less about checking activities off of the project plan and more about "Did the recent work we completed further our goal, why or why not, and what should we do differently going forward?" OKRs shift the organization's mindset toward creating value. The dialogue shifts from what did "I" do previously and what will "I" do next to what did "We" achieve and what should "We" do differently next.

A global consumer packaged goods company sought in 2018 to integrate operations across multiple countries in Central America and the Caribbean. Although the new regional organization was smaller than its peers from a revenue standpoint, it encompassed many more countries, each with its own set of employees, market, and government regulations.

Six months into the shift, signs of trouble emerged. The region's various country managers didn't trust each other and were pulling in different directions. Collaboration across the different subgroups broke down, jeopardizing the region's ability to achieve its goals right out of the gate. Alejandro, the region's new GM, believed the solution lay in getting his direct reports to act as a unified leadership team, focused on the entire region, instead of individual country managers.

Alejandro brought his direct reports together and asked them to share their aspirations for the region and what they needed to do as a leadership team to achieve them. Together, the group came up with three imperatives: shared ownership of business goals, a psychologically safe environment, and a commitment that everyone would be fully present when they met. At the end of the meeting, Alejandro asked everyone to rate the team on a scale of 0 to 10 against each imperative.

The next time they convened, Alejandro shared the results and asked what they could do to improve them. Someone suggested a group norm of not interrupting, and all agreed. As they were finishing the meeting that day, Alejandro again asked them to rate the team against each imperative. "But we just did it," one member protested. Alejandro persisted and started a pattern of collecting data at the end of each meeting and reviewing the results at the start of the next. When the results dipped, they talked about what they might do differently. When the results improved, they asked why. Was it a fluke? Should they do more of what seemed to be working? Over time, the results improved dramatically, not just for the team, but for the business, too.

Alejandro pointed out that sharing the data each time meant the team never lost sight of what was important. They knew where they stood against the goals and could adjust as needed. If they'd just measured results after six months, they wouldn't have accomplished the same thing.

Escaping the Trap

Once upon a time, leaders could analyze a market to understand cause and effect and use the resulting insight to predict what would happen if they pursued a given strategy. Since then, things have become far more complex and faster paced. As a result, up-front strategic planning has become a trap. It promises answers and clarity but delivers disappointment and rigidity. In today's rapidly changing business environment, it's impossible to predict the future with any degree of certainty. Market conditions continually shift, and new threats and opportunities emerge seemingly out of nowhere. Up-front strategic planning simply fails to account for the unpredictable nature of today's business environment.

Rather than relying on static plans and projections, leaders must be willing to experiment, test assumptions, and course correct as needed. In this way they integrate strategy and execution, continually refining strategy and ensuring they're making progress as they go. This requires a willingness to embrace ambiguity and uncertainty, and to prioritize learning and adaptation over rigid adherence to predefined plans. By doing so, leaders can position their organizations to thrive in a fast-changing world, rather than being caught off guard by unexpected challenges or disruptions.

5

Freeing Your People with Purpose-Driven Simple Rules

t was a bold move, but the times called for it. Peter Harmer became CEO of Insurance Australia Group in 2015. The insurance industry was in turmoil following the devastating earthquake in Christchurch, New Zealand, in 2011, and the year-over-year increase in severe bushfires and droughts throughout Australia. The industry kept revisiting actuarial models, premiums, and coverage.

IAG was one of Australia's largest general insurers facing this challenge. After experiencing the devastation, Harmer and his colleagues decided to redefine their organization's purpose. It went from "Helping people manage risk and recover from the hardship of unanticipated loss" to "We make your world a safer place."

As they shared their new aspiration with stakeholders (investors, employees, and customers), many initially pushed back. Investors worried about reduced profitability, employees feared for their jobs, and customers doubted the company could deliver on their bold promise. Harmer and other leaders, however, remained committed, and the new purpose became the lens through which they analyzed and made all decisions.

Guided by the new purpose, frontline staff members changed how they worked as well. Employees were encouraged to bring IAG's new purpose to life in their own context. A host of new initiatives emerged, from crafting policies to meet the specific needs of different customer segments, and working with local governments to create more accurate fire-risk and flood-plain maps, to developing a flame-retardant gel that could be deployed via helicopter to save properties in jeopardy.

Harmer and his colleagues believed that this bold commitment to their purpose wasn't just the right thing to do morally—it would pay off in financial terms. They were right. IAG's profit margin increased, Berkshire Hathaway invested, and employee net promoter scores rose considerably. Moreover, Harmer, who has since retired, attributes the firm's resilience in the face of COVID-19 to how purpose had become deeply embedded in the organization. It kept IAG's employees tightly connected to each other and to customers, providing a "True North" that ensured everyone was pulling in the right direction during disruption.

The Trap of Shareholder Value

Companies and outside critics have talked about organizational purpose for some time, though to little effect. In the 1970s, the prevailing view, articulated eloquently by Milton Friedman in his seminal *New York Times* article, was that businesses existed to increase profits for their owners. That discussion was aimed at public policy; companies, if they had a purpose statement at all, usually resorted to bland language on shareholder value.

That changed in the 2010s, driven by growing understanding of business's interdependence with society, as well as trends such as conscious consumerism, socially responsible investing, and the triple bottom line. Organizational purpose expanded beyond increasing shareholder value toward the impact on multiple stakeholder groups, including employees, partners, and society at large. The Business Roundtable articulated this new approach in 2019 with a revised "Statement on the Purpose of a Corporation." Signed by 181 CEOs from Apple to Walmart, it said that corporations exist for the benefit of all "stakeholders—customers, employees, suppliers, communities, and shareholders."[1]

Even so, companies have struggled to commit to purpose in a practical way. They fall into the trap of seeing purpose as a distraction for business or a constraint that ties the company's hands. To prevent this trap, leaders need to see purpose as a force for creating economic value.

Researchers have found that companies with a clear sense of purpose deliver better financial results, build more commitment from employees, and gain more loyal customers. One study, conducted by *Harvard Business Review* Analytical Services found that companies that operationalize a clear social purpose outperformed the S&P 500 by a factor of 10 between 1996 and 2011.[2] In another cross-industry, six-year study that included 400 public companies, researchers found that companies performed better when mid-level employees believed in the purpose of the organization and understood how to achieve it.[3]

Of course, generating these benefits requires companies to "walk the talk." They cannot simply put a purpose statement on their website. They must embed their purpose in their strategy, business processes, HR practices, decision-making, and culture. In short, the totality of their work must reflect their purpose.

This does not mean blindly pursuing purpose at the expense of profit. Ranjay Gulati, a Harvard Business School professor who has conducted in-depth research in this area, says that the most successful firms balance purpose and profit: "They look beyond short-term, win-win solutions for ones that are good enough for now and promise broader benefits in the future."[4] This work is not easy. It requires that leaders navigate messy trade-off decisions and lean into difficult conversations.

Enterprise software company Red Hat, now a division of IBM, faced just this kind of challenge. In its early days, as Red Hat's revenue soared past $1 billion, the company began hiring executives from larger organizations who had experience rapidly growing operations. Those executives started installing proprietary software systems to manage operations at scale. They were familiar with those systems, after all, and believed them superior to open-source offerings.

Longtime employees were not pleased. Since its inception, Red Hat had promoted openness. Not only did it commercialize open-source software, but it saw its purpose as acting as a catalyst for communities that create better technology the open-source way. Employing proprietary software ran counter to that commitment. The company's Memo List, an internal list-serv, blew up. "Do we not believe in open source? Why are we not using open-source solutions?"

It turned out that the issue was twofold. Not only was the company not using open-source software, but also a small group had made the decision with little input from others. That was the opposite of the open and transparent decision-making approach to which employees were accustomed. According to DeLisa Alexander, the chief people officer at the time, "Anytime at Red Hat that you do something that impacts the culture, you've got to talk about it. You don't just go into a room with your little team and then come out and announce it, unless you want to blow things up."[5] For Red Hat, open source wasn't just a strategy for developing software; it involved a deep-seated belief in the power of communities to add value. Proprietary software systems challenged that moral commitment, especially when installed by top-down management.

So Alexander responded the Red Hat way. She pulled together the fighting factions and said, "Let's do a redo. What would it look like if we did this right and we were really successful?" Ultimately, the team determined that proprietary software was in fact the right approach for Red Hat in certain circumstances. Through their discussions the team also created the Open Decision framework, with tools for making transparent, inclusive decisions in organizations that embrace open-source principles. Red Hat ended up publicizing these guidelines, which multiple organizations have since adopted. By respecting its foundational purpose, Red Hat found a path forward that sustained its mission of building open communities, which continued even after the acquisition by IBM.

Purpose as a Compass in Complex Environments

A strong corporate purpose was a nice-to-have in the era of stability, which is why many companies didn't bother to articulate one. Annual reports and other communications often included support for environmental or social causes, but this was window dressing and employees knew it.

That world no longer exists for most companies. Whether they like it or not, they're operating amid turmoil and rapid change. To thrive in this environment, companies must continually adapt, and those with a clear sense of purpose are better able to do just that. In one study that included close to 500 global leaders, researchers found that "executives who treat purpose as a core driver of strategy and decision-making reported greater ability to drive successful innovation and transformational change."[6]

A clear purpose helps organizations deal with complexity in multiple ways. It serves as a North Star when markets become confusing or chaotic. When the best course of action isn't clear, multiple interests are competing for attention, or people can't wait for clarity from up high, an operationalized purpose guides the organization in a single right direction.

That's what Tom Bigda-Peyton found during the COVID-19 pandemic, when he served as chief learning officer for Catholic Health, an integrated network of hospitals on Long Island: "At least every other month we had to deal with a new disruption that we weren't prepared for. Each time, we leaned into the organization's mission. It anchored us and kept us focused on the most important things when we might otherwise have gotten lost."

Purpose also supports collaboration. Organizations that dynamically rewire themselves around purpose become complex adaptive systems that respond well to threats or opportunities. They rapidly modify how groups and functions share information, solve problems, and make decisions, so they can tap the right expertise, develop solutions, and execute faster. Without a common purpose, too often subgroups are stuck in different agendas and assumptions. They struggle to connect and collaborate, because they can't see eye to eye.

When different groups share a common purpose, they have a solid foundation on which to build their relationship. In one instance, we were consulting with the vice president for manufacturing at a mid-sized industrial company. He was struggling to get resources for an initiative, but the colleague in charge of the resources wasn't going along. The colleague wanted to help, but the initiative just wasn't on his list of priorities. When the VP reframed the initiative in the context of the organization's broader purpose, however, his colleague recognized the connection to his own priorities. He became excited about the project and reallocated his team accordingly.

Purpose also fosters employee autonomy. In complex environments, there isn't time for employees to report back to leaders and wait for instructions. Circumstances change too quickly. As a result, employees must be ready to act on their own. Purpose supports this goal by serving as a form of simple rules. It provides employees with an understanding of the organization's broader interests while equipping them to make decisions and act locally. That's what research consultancy Contexis found in another study: "Where we see organizations with a clearly understood and authentic purpose, we see remarkable levels of clarity of strategy and objectives, remarkable velocity of decision-making, and exceptional adaptability."[7]

In complexity science, simple rules define the space between order and disorder. When leaders prescribe what everyone must do and how they do it, the system becomes too ordered; it lacks the flexibility to adapt to rapidly changing conditions. Alternatively, when leaders provide no guidance, the system lacks structure. Simple rules balance the two extremes. They enable creativity and collaboration to flourish in a way that fits the organization's needs.

Early in Yahoo!'s life cycle, the firm's development managers adhered to four simple rules: know the priority rank of each product in development, ensure that every engineer can work on every project, maintain the Yahoo! look in the user interface, and launch products quietly. Software developers could modify products however they saw fit, as long as they followed these guidelines. One developer decided on his own to stay up all night building a new web page dedicated to the European soccer championships, which quickly became Yahoo!'s most popular page. Because he understood the rules, he was able to pursue a great idea in the moment.[8]

Leaders often say they want to empower employees, but they fear what might happen if they do. What if people focus on the wrong things or run off in different directions? How do resources get allocated among everyone who asks for them? Purpose, in conjunction with a set of simple rules, creates guard rails to help coordinate and ensure everyone is pulling in the same direction.

Jorgen Vig Knudstorp, the executive chairman and former CEO of the Lego Group, led the way in revitalizing the brand in the 2010s. He saw firsthand the benefit of equipping employees with the knowledge to act autonomously. He said one of his most important jobs was telling employees, "Thank you for doing all the things I never told you to do." He added that "you shouldn't run a company based on what you tell [employees] to do. You should run it based on intention. The way I put it is that 'context setting' is more important than controlling."[9] Coordinated by common purpose, or what Vig Knudstorp refers to as context, the disparate parts of the organization can work autonomously and still achieve coherent results.

A strong purpose has the added benefit of engaging employees. People have an inherent need for meaningful work, and in companies with a strong purpose, they report that their work is more meaningful.[10] This sense of meaning can provide more motivation than hopes for a salary raise or a bonus plan. We need look only at the extraordinary effort people voluntarily expend on causes or social movements that they believe in.

A strong purpose thus frees leaders from having to micromanage (and thereby demoralize) employees during disruptive times. The Contexis researchers also found that "Leadership teams that activate purpose in their culture result in a net gain in productive employee behaviors of between 25 and 40%, and a similar uplift in retention."[11]

When people connect their work to a broader purpose, they'll push through obstacles and act with courage. They'll kick in the attention and creativity to address the sudden challenges that complexity serves up. They'll share information with colleagues, collaborate across the organization, and make plans happen—maybe not as envisioned, but better. You won't need to tell people what to do, which is a good thing because in complex environments, you don't have the bandwidth to do that anyway. Employees will capture perishable opportunities in ways you never could in headquarters. It's one of the reasons that Joe Robles, retired army major general and former CEO of USAA, maintains that a leader's most important job is connecting people to their purpose.

Finally, concerned by governments' apparent inability to provide lasting solutions, people are looking to companies to address societal challenges. Edelman, a global communication firm, surveyed 36,000 people in 28 countries and found that businesses are four times more likely to gain consumer trust by taking on social issues.[12] Additionally, more than half of all Americans now say that they would switch brands based on the brand's stance on social and political issues.[13]

Companies with a defined purpose have an advantage, and it's not just a reputation for social responsibility. Even if your organization has been fortunate enough to avoid being dragged into a social media storm on an issue, a strong purpose provides a rationale for tough decisions. The purpose not only increases transparency but also builds credibility. Even those who don't agree with the final decision—and in today's complex world it's often not possible to please everyone—have to acknowledge that the company acted with integrity. Purpose provides a compass with which to navigate thorny issues.

An example was Starbucks' response to the 2018 arrest of two Black men in one of their Philadelphia coffeeshops. A core part of the chain's purpose is creating a welcoming environment, and it had failed. The CEO flew to the city for a formal apology, and then shut 8,000 coffeeshops for a day for sensitivity training. The chain also changed its policy to ensure that anyone could sit in their cafes or use their restrooms even without buying anything.[14]

Why Leaders Fall Short

Despite broad recognition of its value, most leaders fail to promote a strong shared purpose. As a result, fewer than a third of employees feel fully connected to the purpose and identity of their organization.[15] In our experience, leaders fall short for several reasons.

The first is that leaders do not appreciate the power of a shared purpose. Some see purpose as "touchy-feely," while others perceive the organization in economic terms and view people as acting only out of self-interest. These views can amount to a self-fulfilling prophecy. As business school professors Robert Quinn and Anjan Thakor point out, these leaders set highly transactional expectations, and employees end up acting in accordance with the incentives and controls imposed on them.[16] Instead of seeing opportunities, everyone in the organization ends up focusing on material costs and rewards in a zero-sum situation. They feel conflict, resist feedback, underperform, and stagnate. Managers believe their assumptions were correct and double down on the extrinsic incentives, which leads employees to pay even less attention to hard-to-measure activities such as mentorship and collaboration. People do only what they have to do. Results fall short of expectations, and frustrated managers clamp down further.

Some leaders go to the other extreme, articulating lofty purposes that don't reflect what their organization actually does. For example, back in 2000, BP rebranded itself from British Petroleum to "Beyond Petroleum." Rather than maximize the sustainable delivery of affordable fossil fuels, the company promised to hold emissions constant and act as a steward of the planet. Six years later a BP oil pipeline leak caused one of the largest oil spills in Alaska's history. Then in 2010, its Deepwater Horizon rig exploded, resulting in the largest marine oil spill in history—and widespread charges of hypocrisy.

Likewise, WeWork, the shared space provider, famously aimed to "elevate the world's consciousness." Shortly before going public, the company collapsed and survived only by being bought, with the departing CEO accused of self-enrichment. When purpose statements overpromise, they suggest that the company isn't grounded in what customers actually want. They ring hollow and arouse skepticism rather than inspire stakeholders.

Indeed, many companies practice what Gulati calls "convenient purpose." Their statements of purpose or mission, no matter how noble, are mere window dressing rarely operationalized into day-to-day practices. When the going gets tough, these organizations revert to a profit-first strategy. Employees become cynical, and the very purpose statements intended to inspire them actually reduce engagement.

We know of one educational nonprofit whose purpose focused on learning. Yet when any employees made a mistake, the leaders responded harshly. Despite the organization's mission, the leaders didn't see the inevitable miscues as learning opportunities. Their approach made employees less likely to take chances in responding to emerging developments.

Uncovering Your Compelling Purpose

Discovering your organization's purpose isn't easy. It requires simultaneously addressing the interests of customers, employees, communities, suppliers, shareholders, and the environment. Often, this means making uncomfortable trade-offs. But, as we saw in the case of Red Hat, purpose-driven companies are willing to engage in this messy work.

Leaders seeking a strong purpose need to uncover it, not invent it. Most organizations have a compelling purpose deep down that can be found through self-reflection and hard work. One way to go about it comes from the Japanese concept of *ikigai* (ee-key-guy), or "a reason for being." Made up of the terms *iki*, meaning "alive" or "life" and *gai*, meaning "benefit" or "worth," ikigai appears as a Venn diagram with four overlapping spheres: what you love, what you're good at, what the world needs, and what you can get paid for. Those who exist at

the center of these spheres experience meaning, purpose, and fulfill-
ment in life while contributing to the good of others. Although ikigai
started for individuals, leaders can use the same framework to uncover
their organization's purpose. (See Figure 5.1.)

If your company's ikigai doesn't readily appear, one source of
inspiration can be thinking about how your organization responds in
times of crisis. Another, as Gulati points out, is the company's founding: "Deep purpose leaders look to the past, immersing themselves
in the intentions of founders and early employees, scouring for
themes that capture the firm's ineffable soul or essence." Basing the
purpose on the founding yields authenticity that results "in deeper
emotional connections and more commitment to the reason for
being." It also "serves as a bridge to the future, helping leaders to
chart a path ahead that is meaningful, coherent, and grounded."[17]

You can't define your company's purpose, however, just by looking
through the rearview mirror. Although it's important for purpose to
be rooted in the organization's experience, purpose must be forward
looking as well, encompassing the organization's aspirations for
the future.

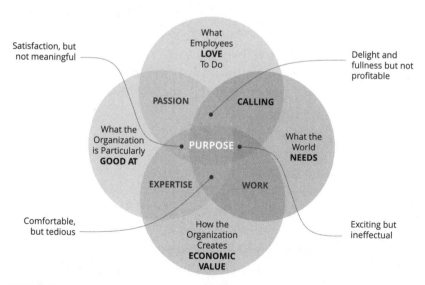

FIGURE 5.1   Ikigai for organizations

Another source can be customers themselves. After hearing from many customers about the fond memories of using its products to repair machines with family members, WD-40 adopted the purpose of creating "positive lasting memories solving problems in factories, homes and workshops around the world."

Note that an organization's purpose can come in different flavors. Many companies focus their purpose statements on how the firm benefits society. For example, CVS's purpose is "helping people on their path to better health." Other companies focus their purpose on how they run their business. Charles Schwab, for example, seeks "to champion every client's goals with passion and integrity." Still others set their purpose on the value of their products or services. Google, for instance, famously set out to "organize the world's information."

Whatever your company's purpose, a broad set of stakeholders should agree to it. Otherwise, purpose becomes mere performance, something imposed on the rest of the organization without broad acceptance. Even better, involve those stakeholders early in the process. They'll be more likely to rally around a purpose that they helped to uncover.

Overall, your company's purpose should be powerful (compelling to employees), authentic (ringing true to insiders), credible (the company can follow through), instructive (helping employees navigate ambiguity), and simple (easy to understand). If you develop it with a range of colleagues, not just other executives, you'll improve your odds of success.

Making Purpose Real

Discovering your company's purpose is just the first step. Leaders need to resist the temptation to treat a noble purpose like a bumper sticker, slapped on and then forgotten. Even big events have little impact without follow-through. We know one executive who's seen purpose announcements so stylized she calls them *kabuki*, a self-conscious, grandiose performance for its own sake. These performances satisfy the leaders' need for a well-publicized mission, and perhaps even some employees' need for a desirable vision, but they have little effect on actual operations.

Employees must feel that that the purpose is "ours," that it is inherent in the organization. This means connecting them to it through ongoing interaction and dialogue. Leaders must relentlessly drive the purpose home. The biggest difference between companies that successfully prioritize purpose and those that do not is communication from leadership.

Ortho Clinical Diagnostics, a maker of medical devices, addressed this challenge head-on. After Ortho spun out from a much larger corporation, CEO Martin Maudaus wanted employees to understand their connection to the purpose of the new, independent firm. He commissioned a series of real-world case studies highlighting examples of Ortho employees going above and beyond to bring to life the company's purpose of improving and saving lives with diagnostics. At each Ortho location he used the case studies to spark conversations with employees about decisions and actions they might have taken in those instances. He closed each session asking participants to commit to a single action they would take to promote the company's purpose going forward.

Another tactic comes from Eisai, a global pharmaceutical company. Eisai urges every employee to spend two to three days each year interacting with and learning from patients. The experience connects employees to the company's purpose of "improving the health of all individuals worldwide regardless of wealth or geography." CEO Haruo Naito points out that "we get to know how patients feel by spending time with them, which eventually moves all of us to tears. Our motivation comes from our desire to do something about the true needs we grasped then and there."[18]

Beyond connecting employees to the company's purpose, leaders must embed the purpose throughout the organization. PayPal, for example, seeks to "democratize financial services to ensure that everyone, regardless of background or economic standing, has access to affordable, convenient, and secure products and services to take control of their financial lives." Like a doctor caring for his or her own family's health, the company surveys its employees on their financial wellness. It develops and tracks metrics such as "net disposable income" and takes steps to boost financial security as needed. In 2019 it raised minimum wages, lowered the cost of medical benefits, gave stock to all employees, and trained people in financial wellness— all to enable people to participate in financial services.[19]

Part of the job of leaders is holding themselves and others accountable for living the company's purpose. The stated purpose of science-led, data intelligence company CorEvitas is to "advance patient care by generating real-world insights into health conditions and therapeutics." Essential to that purpose is collaboration; CorEvitas puts "team ahead of individual." But what happens when the firm has high-performing employees who regularly demean their colleagues?

Those can be tough calls, especially in a tight talent market, and when the people involved play a critical role in the company's operations. But as CEO Ray Hill points out, "Culture is what you're willing to tolerate." So he let go of high performers who couldn't or wouldn't change. It was worth the substantial short-term pain. "I think people really pay attention to that stuff, because if they see someone like that leave all of a sudden, wow, maybe the company is serious about changing the culture here." But Hill and other executives also held themselves accountable. The experience reminded them that novice managers need training on how to give feedback in respectful ways.[20]

Similarly, Garry Ridge, who recently retired after decades as CEO of WD-40, believes that leaders are responsible for building a "culture of belonging" that fosters commitment to the company's purpose. Ridge had told the organization early in his term as CEO that if the company had to let go of an employee because it had failed to develop that employee's skills, he would fire the senior-most person in that department. Soon he learned that someone had indeed been dismissed. When he asked for that employee's development plan, he found out the plan didn't exist. So he kept his promise and fired the executive overseeing that division.

A difficult lesson, yes, but Ridge was committed to walking the talk. Moreover, he doesn't only hold others accountable. He keeps a sticky note on both his computer and in his notebook that asks the questions, "Am I being the person I want to be right now?" and "Who is that person?" According to Ridge, "Turbulence makes it easy to get pulled off the path and into the bushes and that's very damaging. I have to keep reminding myself of who I want to be."[21] These are just some of the ways companies can embrace their purpose. The goal here is not just to boost employee engagement, however important that is. A common purpose enables companies to thrive in a complex world where people must make decisions in the moment, rather than waiting for approval from higher-ups.

Escaping the Trap

Leaders often resist championing a strong, shared purpose because they either don't believe it adds value or they fear being boxed in. Accordingly, they pay lip service to purpose. This approach worked when leaders had the luxury of making all the big decisions and could instruct everyone else on what to do. But in a faster, more disruptive age, ignoring purpose in favor of "getting work done" is a trap.

Employees, customers, partners, even competitors now have access to a voluminous amount of information about how any company does business. Companies that don't demonstrate their stated purpose through their actions are quickly found out and breed cynicism. More important, in rapidly changing environments, leaders don't have time to make all the pressing decisions themselves. Armed with a strong sense of purpose, employees have an organizational compass that equips them to act autonomously in real time.

What's more, as Red Hat shows, a strong purpose doesn't have to prevent companies from doing what the business requires. It can guide organizations without becoming a straitjacket. All it takes is sustained leadership to uncover and promote an authentic commitment, and then truly walk the talk. That commitment, as IAG shows, can then lead to unexpected opportunities and advances in the marketplace. Constraints can actually generate creativity and yield new opportunities.

Developing that purpose also illuminates a central challenge of this book. Companies need leaders to initiate a process of discovery and propagation—while still ensuring that purpose is owned by the entire organization, not imposed top-down. Leaders who congratulate themselves for developing a strong purpose—not the showy, superficial values that motivate no one—must resist an ego-driven, heroic posture as the great discoverer of the ideal mission. Purpose making, like strategy and other key elements, must be informed by the entire organization and spread naturally. Leaders need to facilitate that work while keeping the focus on the company, not themselves.

6 Why Community Organizers Consistently Beat Superheroes

Many of us grew up fantasizing about being the hero who saves the day. Whether it is the sheriff who captures the villain, the superhero saving Earth, the Jedi destroying the Death Star, or the basketball player making the winning shot, we imagine ourselves as invaluable, the answer to others' prayers. Relatedly, many of us yearn for a hero to solve our problems and make things right without us taking risks or shouldering a heavy cost. The media loves to put leaders on a pedestal and grant them iconic status. Some leaders take advantage of this desire and make claims such as "I alone can fix it." Many more feel pressure to be the invincible leader.

But the fantasy is a trap. In reality, creating and leading organizations that thrive amidst disruption requires less individual heroism than many leaders believe. It's far better to be a systems enabler, akin to a community organizer, who activates others.

Former US President Barack Obama's campaign opponents ridiculed him for working as a community organizer early in his career. In fact, his experiences on the South Side of Chicago were invaluable in preparing him for the presidency. He learned about grassroots organizing and building coalitions. He had to work with diverse groups of people to identify problems and develop solutions without telling anyone what to do.

The experience taught him to communicate with and mobilize people toward a common goal. Working with low-income communities also gave him a firsthand understanding of the challenges those groups face, which informed his policy decisions as president. His ability to bring people together and inspire hope actually led others to call him a hero.

But what about the world of corporations, government, and health care delivery? Catholic Health, a health care system including six hospitals on New York's Long Island, had long been managed with a directive, top-down style. When the COVID-19 pandemic hit, however, senior leaders recognized that the situation called for a new approach. Requirements regarding personal protective equipment (PPE) were constantly shifting and, at one point, PPE was in short supply. Meanwhile the influx of COVID patients dramatically increased the need for health care workers with respiratory expertise.

As it became clear that existing policies needed to be adapted, the leaders looked to people on the front line for guidance. According to Tom Bigda-Peyton, Catholic Health's chief learning officer during the pandemic, "It was a paradigm shift. Recognizing that they didn't have the answers, leaders had to leave their title at the door, reach out, and ask for help." Once engaged, Catholic Health's employees worked together in remarkable ways. One group came up with new PPE guidelines that allowed providers to treat patients while staying safe. Another developed a buddy system to rapidly train colleagues on new approaches and ensure no one felt alone. Yet another created resiliency training in 15-minute increments for frontline practitioners.

As a result of these efforts, Catholic Health sent 16,000 patients back to their families from hospitals, and provided care to 19,000 additional patients that prevented hospitalization. According to Dr. Patrick O'Shaughnessy, CEO of Catholic Health, "During the pandemic everyone stepped up, they worked extra, they delivered in the face of a clinical challenge that has not been seen in over 100 years. And it's because of them, not me, that we have those kinds of statistics to share."[1] Most leaders learned to succeed by boldly committing or withholding resources and by swooping in to fix problems. But that heroism makes sense only when environments are fairly predictable, which is no longer true of most industries. You might dash in to fight a battle that's suddenly moved to another field. But even if the battle is still there, you're fighting without a diversity of perspectives that enable you to develop a good plan of attack. Your efforts generate no engagement or ownership from the rest of your team, and you risk burning out from the ongoing strain of effort.

When you make decisions alone, you gratify your ego, but you're relying on partial information. Ignorant like Icarus, you fly too close to the sun. Leaders need a new approach that engages everyone to solve problems.

Temptations of Heroism

The corporate pursuit of heroism is certainly understandable. Companies began worshipping at the cult of the leader in the 1990s, elevating individuals at the expense of organizational effectiveness. It's hard to forget that period, when CEO Michael Eisner of Disney was winning accolades and enormous pay packages. Some employees quipped that with such a big pay disparity, they might as well just sit around and wait for him to meet the company's challenges.[2]

A similar process has unfolded with the founders of startups. We want to ascribe mystical powers to these leaders. In a profile of Theranos founder Elizabeth Holmes, Ken Auletta describes her as "unnervingly serene," someone who speaks in a "near whisper" and drinks only smoothies made from green vegetables.[3] It's suggested that this other worldliness helped explain her accomplishments, such as designing a time machine at the age of seven, reading *Moby Dick* at nine, and completing three years of college-level Mandarin before she finished high school. Similarly, Apple founder Steve Jobs, Twitter cofounder Jack Dorsey, and Zappos founder Tony Hsieh have all been described as shaman-like, flaunting self-deprivation and subsisting on strict diets.[4]

We've built up our leaders so much that many of them feel both entitled and impelled to justify their exalted position. Anyone who rises to leadership positions almost inevitably has a great deal of ambition, often with an accompanying need to validate their own amazingness. As leaders have gotten outsized attention, those needs for personal validation have taken off—just when organizations need everyone working together.

Similar to Merrill Lynch's John Thain before the 2008 financial crisis, some leaders seek lavish offices and the trappings of wealth and power on the rationale that a grand presence will confirm their authority. They seek to control every situation and to project an image that they add more value than anyone else. But in the long run they're only as good as their team. True heroism in leadership lies in subordinating your ego to the organization's success, especially when complexity and uncertainty prevent you from tackling every crisis head-on.

Companies do need leaders to intervene heroically at times, and act decisively to right the ship. We saw some of that at the beginning of the pandemic in spring 2020, when leaders had to make tough decisions on furloughs. And we've seen it in Ukraine, when the country's president, Volodymyr Zelensky, stepped up unexpectedly to rally the country and its allies following Russia's invasion. But it should happen rarely. Frequent interventions bring on burnout for the leader and frustration for everyone else.

More important, people don't feel ownership and responsibility for anything unless they help to create it. No matter how charismatic, a leader's heroism is inherently disempowering. It creates a culture of dependence. And that's fatal in a company striving to become a complex adaptive system where everyone must act independently. Leaders need information and activism from the group, but it's hard to feel autonomous when your boss is dashing around fixing things.

Heroism also creates a subtle but important problem of scope. In order to gratify egos, leaders feel tempted to set spectacular stretch goals that capture everyone's imagination. Setting a goal is easy, and it gives leaders a sense of accomplishment. Indeed, many see goal setting as a core function of leadership. But goals are not what distinguishes performance. What matters is the system that leaders put in place to achieve the goal. Heroic leaders focus their energy on achieving a specific goal, but that's dangerous in unpredictable environments where the shifting landscape suddenly creates new imperatives. Goal-oriented heroes also have fragile motivation: either they achieve the goal and are done or fail to achieve it and despair.

It's far better, as James Clear, author of *Atomic Habits*, has argued, to make goals secondary to creating an effective system of habits. The aim here is for people to continue to improve over time, regardless of failures or accomplishments along the way. Heroes are great at singular accomplishments, not so good at instilling the ordinary habits that gradually and sustainably bring success. With circumstances continually changing, goals can distract us from these shifts. Good habits, guided by a few simple rules, are a far better investment.

Even seemingly innocuous instincts can get leaders in trouble, especially if their colleagues are used to a more participative approach. Former chief people officer at Red Hat (now part of IBM) DeLisa Alexander originally joined the company as assistant general counsel focused on intellectual property rights. One of her first assignments was to select the right open-source license for a particular piece of software. After doing her own research, she told her colleagues, "Here's the license you're going to use." To which they collectively and vehemently disagreed.

Her immediate reaction was "I'm the expert here. If I were outside counsel, you would've paid me a lot of money to come up with this answer, and you would've run with it." After gaining some emotional distance from the decision, and managing her ego, she realized that the engineers knew a lot about open-source practices and that they brought tremendous insight. Coming to the right solution required listening and collaboration.

As she recalls, "I went from being the lawyer, command-and-control, I've got all the answers, why aren't you listening to me; to,

I don't really have to do anything but spot the issues, and you may spot them too, that's great. I'm part of a team, trying to come to the right solution."[5]

In complex environments, leaders must let go of the idea that they have all the answers, that they alone can solve the problem. That's a path to suboptimization and exhaustion. Instead, leaders must act as an orchestrator for the broader organization. Similar to a catalyst in a chemical reaction, a leader's job is to amplify and accelerate the efforts of others. They must evolve from "sage on the stage" to "guide on the side."

Organizational theorist Henry Mintzberg calls the latter style *communityship*.[6] Unlike traditional business leadership, which Mintzberg considers "egocentric," communityship emphasizes involvement with others and fostering a culture that encourages personal initiative. This approach counteracts both micromanagement and the use of top-down authority by remote leaders, known as *macro leading*. The benefits of communityship can be observed in many successful open-source organizations such as Wikipedia and Mozilla.

Overcoming Egos

Leaders can take a variety of steps to discourage heroism in themselves and in the people around them. The first is to cultivate humility.

In competitive markets, success usually depends on soberly assessing opportunities and carefully investing resources. But leaders are still human beings with egos. If you lead a business unit, you just can't help but become protective of your turf and your subordinates. It's easy to take your authority personally and to want to validate it through heroic acts. When you equate your self-worth with your position, it changes how you respond to challenges.

In fact, the higher you rise, the more your position becomes part of your identity—and not necessarily in a good way. The greater your responsibilities, the more time you devote to your position and the less to your family, community, and other parts of your life. If you're in the C-suite, then you're expected to be available almost 24/7, which means downplaying most of your life outside work.

What's more, others change how they relate to you. They're eager to please, quick to agree with your opinions and laugh at your jokes. Your ego grows. Jonathan Davidson, psychiatry and behavioral science professor at Duke University, and his coauthor call this the *hubris syndrome*.[7]

Those big egos, in turn, make us susceptible to manipulation. According to Rasmus Houggard, founder and CEO of Potential Project, "When we're a victim of our own need to be seen as great, we end up being led into making decisions that may be detrimental to ourselves, our people, and our organization."[8]

An inflated ego also makes us less likable, which undermines our relationships. When we see ourselves as the hero, others' feedback feels like criticism. We know one leader who was so eager to be perceived as smart that he would spend an inordinate amount of time working on projects, hoping that others would acknowledge his brilliance. When he got constructive comments, his first reaction was, "How dare you! Can't you see it's perfect? I worked on this for hours."

Even others' initiative or success can be threatening. Instead of colleagues, they become rebels challenging your success. The thought process becomes "Who needs me if my people can act so forthrightly without me? Am I adding enough value? Maybe I'm actually an impostor?" Likewise, when you swoop in to save the day on a difficult project, you confirm that the universe was right to put you in charge.

We're not suggesting that leaders should reject their egos. We can no more escape our egos than our shadows. Our egos help us balance our own needs with those of others. This integration is critical in making decisions, taking risks, and handling criticism. Our ego also enables us to connect with our organization's sense of purpose (discussed in Chapter 5). Without an ego we wouldn't take pride in or be inspired by our company's mission to improve patients' lives, protect the planet, or achieve breakthrough innovation.

A healthy ego balances self-confidence with humility. Leaders become aware of their strengths and their weaknesses and act accordingly. They recognize that their value doesn't stem from their intelligence or even being needed by others. They aim to make their people self-sufficient so they, the leaders, can expand their impact in new ways.

In a meta-analysis of research into ego development, researchers determined that one's ego develops through four stages.[9] In the first, self-centeredness, our focus is on "what do I think is important?" From there, the ego evolves through group-centeredness (i.e., "How can I fit into the group"), to independence (i.e., "I'm in control of my own destiny"), and ultimately to group affiliation. In this final stage of development, the ego's focus shifts to "How can I, amid constant change and disruption, become self-actualized while also demonstrating to others how to make their own way?" We feel comfortable with ambiguity and the innate complexity of real people and situations. The researchers sharply distinguish that focus from the narcissism and arrogance common in earlier stages, arguing that people with strong egos can channel their emotions to productive ends.

Leaders can develop healthy egos in several ways. One is to avoid comparing themselves to others, which results in competition, insecurity, or overconfidence. If leaders feel the need to compare, it should be to their own personal goals and aspirations. Leaders can also surround themselves with people willing to speak truth to power. Truth tellers not only improve decision-making and generate creative ideas but also keep the leader grounded and accountable.

The act of learning also keeps us humble. Learning requires an acknowledgment that we have room to grow. This goes for everyone, including the CEO. As Indra Nooyi, CEO of PepsiCo from 2006 to 2018, remarked, "Just because you are CEO, don't think you have landed. You must continually increase your learning, the way you think, and the way you approach the organization. I've never forgotten that."[10]

This learning can come in many forms: taking on a new role, reading, formal training, and listening to podcasts and webinars. One of the best ways leaders learn is through unstructured interactions with others. Verizon, for example, brings together small cohorts of leaders from across the enterprise to learn and coach each other for six months. Reverse mentoring, in which a leader is mentored by a more junior employee, is a particularly powerful way of learning while keeping your ego in check. Daisy Gray, vice president at P&G, used the practice twice. When she moved to Russia to lead P&G's beauty care business she received mentoring from a junior colleague to learn the workplace culture in Russia. Later, she chose to have a category manager reverse-mentor her, to help her understand the shopping habits of millennials. "It's not the biggest age gap," Gray says, "but there is a chasm in how we operate online."[11]

Leaders can cultivate humility by making it a daily practice to reflect on the individuals and factors that contributed to their success. By recognizing the role of others, they can prevent their success from leading to an inflated ego. To reinforce this perspective, they should conclude the reflection by expressing gratitude to those who helped them along the way.

One element of corporate life that discourages humility is the abundance of perks that come with senior positions. We know of leaders who enjoy having their own personal driver, luxurious offices far removed from the masses, and private entrances. They can work days at a time without meeting anyone new. Such privileges might feel good, but they're ultimately imprisoning. By contrast, when DoubleClick moved to a new building, CEO Kevin Ryan purposely took one of the smallest offices, centrally located near much of the company's critical activity. His decision shut down the jockeying for offices by other executives and set a tone of collegiality and collaboration. Ryan wanted to be like Henry V rallying the troops for collective success, not Luke Skywalker on his own journey fighting the empire.

Strength in Numbers

Treating others as valuable contributors not only discourages heroism but also creates better results. Walt Rakowich, the former CEO of Prologis, learned this the hard way. He had risen to his position at the industrial real estate company in 2008 only after the board had fired his predecessor for running the company into the ground. A few months in, the company was still teetering on the edge of bankruptcy.

At a crucial meeting with his leadership team, Rakowich called a break. He went for a walk—and promptly fainted from the intense stress. Although he quickly regained consciousness, he still had no solution. When the meeting resumed, all he could manage was, "I don't know what to do" and "I need your help."

His plea was a turning point, prompting other executives to rally around him. With a lot of diligence, creative thinking, and luck, the team figured out how to buy enough time with creditors to turn around the business. When Rakowich retired in 2013, Prologis was solidly profitable and the biggest firm in the industry.

Seeking to benefit from everyone's contributions, one of the most successful private equity companies we've encountered has purposefully built an ecosystem characterized by information-sharing and collaboration. The firm takes great pains to hire the best talent, but as one executive told us, "Once you're in you're in. There is no hazing. It's highly collaborative. Everyone has a voice, including the newest associate. It's never one person on the chopping block if something goes poorly, or one person celebrating success if it goes well. Everyone is in it together."

Many leaders struggle to incorporate the breadth of knowledge and expertise that exists within their company. This is often because they haven't learned to effectively delegate. That's a shame: they're leaving tremendous value on the table, according to a study of dozens of *Inc.* 500 CEOs that found faster growth and greater revenue in companies whose leaders delegated.[12] In many cases, it's the leader's own hesitancy that keeps them from delegating. The list of reasons is long: I can do it faster myself; my staff members already have too much on their plates; I can't risk that it won't be done well; I don't want to lose visibility on what's going on; doing this work is how I add value; and if I give this responsibility up, I'll have to focus on stuff I don't want to do.

Each of those reasons may be true, but if leaders want to do many things well and make a big impact, they need to delegate. Leaders who need inspiration can look to the legendary Warren Buffett. The "Oracle of Omaha" learned to keep his hands off his portfolio of companies. He and his partners focus on buying and selling companies, and then selecting and compensating executives to run them on their own.

One way for leaders to surmount the delegation hurdle is to recognize that it's not an either-or decision. There are lots of shades of gray between doing the work yourself and handing it off entirely. Leaders can solicit input from others, work in partnership with others, or delegate with informed guidance. The context of the situation should dictate the approach.

One piece of the puzzle is the decision of whom to delegate to. This isn't just about who can do it. Leaders should also consider who needs to develop the associated skills, who has enough bandwidth, who has shown interest, and who is ready for a new challenge. Successful delegators can articulate why they chose whom they did. They are also explicit with the delegatee about what they hope to achieve, why it's important, what resources are available, what approaches they recommend, and the quality of output they expect.

Sharing the Spotlight

When asking others to help, it's important to acknowledge their contribution. The best leaders are quick to share credit. Carl Bennet led the turnaround of Getinge AB, a maker of medical equipment, after acquiring it from Electrolux, but he downplays his role. His main contribution, he said, was to unleash the power of employees to do what needed to be done and to remain committed to the company no matter how much trouble it met. "It was a great company just waiting for someone to care about it," Bennet modestly said.[13]

Leaders can also curtail heroism by amplifying others' voices. We've all witnessed situations when a colleague's great idea went unnoticed or was attributed to someone else. One study validates the frequency of this phenomenon. Researchers participated in 78 team meetings and found that groups frequently overlooked ideas that members suggested. If they revived those ideas later, they sometimes gave credit to the wrong person.[14] This lack of attribution can be particularly troubling for people from traditionally disadvantaged populations who are more likely to be overlooked.

Leaders can combat this tendency by amplifying the voices of others. In another study of 2,760 participants, researchers found that when leaders deliberately call attention to others' ideas, making sure to give proper credit, the influence of those who voiced the ideas increases.[15] What's more, in a true win-win, the practice raised the status of the leader and other endorsers along with that of the originator.

When you're the hero, everyone looks to you. You become the focal point. Although gratifying, this attention dampens creativity and collaboration. People stop generating their own ideas or paying attention to one another, because they wonder whether they're in sync with your ideas and supporting your agenda. Leaders can fight this tendency by shining the spotlight on others, especially those who might be marginalized. They can publicly champion their successes and endorse their ideas.

From Crisis to Cause

During a crisis, it's common to want a hero to save the day. Heroes perform daring acts of bravery, but they tend to ride off into the sunset when the immediate threat has passed. By contrast, facilitating leaders work with and through others to create lasting change.

Although heroes are often judged by their personal achievements, the true measure of a leader's success lies in the commitment and effectiveness of followers. Leaders don't just solve current problems; they also build better futures.

When COVID-19 hit, Garry Ridge was CEO of WD-40 (he retired in 2022). He sought to strengthen the company as well as address the challenges. The pandemic led to a sharp increase in demand for Lysol—which made it harder to secure aerosol cans, a key component in WD-40s product line. Then the harsh Texas winter storm of February 2021 disrupted shipping for weeks. Demand for WD-40s products remained strong, due to remote workers renovating their homes, but without product, the demand meant little.

Rather than reactively swoop in to address those challenges, Ridge kept the company focused on the big picture with three core priorities: protecting the safety and the well-being of employees, servicing customers as well as possible, and protecting the core of the business so it could thrive when the pandemic ended.

Ridge didn't go it alone. He assembled a global strategic council, which met most days to deal with the ongoing developments. At times it included close to 100 participants from 17 countries. Together, Ridge and his colleagues kept asking themselves the same questions: "Why do we believe what we believe at this moment?" And then, "What should we do, what could we do, and what will we do?" The process was a form of sensemaking (discussed in Chapter 7) that created a shared understanding throughout the company—and then much greater unity when the company did shift its product mix and supply chains. The result: 2021 was WD-40s most successful year in its history.

In a crisis, people come together. They do amazing things, but when the crisis ends, they go back to their silos. If leaders want to truly change the operating model, they need to reframe the crisis as a cause that people can rally behind over the long term.

Leaders do this by shifting the focus from immediate problems to a shared purpose. This gives everyone space to step up and be a hero.

Decentralization: The Power of We

Leaders can further reduce heroism through structural changes. Decentralization reverses the corporate tendency to put enormous power in the hands of a few. Leaders can better resist hero syndrome, while employees feel greater ownership and responsibility for outcomes.

As we write this, the downsides of a hero-led organization are obvious in Russia's invasion of Ukraine. As we pointed out in Chapter 1, Russia is a centralized, authoritarian regime with power concentrated in President Vladimir Putin. When Putin launched the full-scale attack in February 2022, he anticipated a rapid and decisive victory that would secure his place in Russian history. In fact, his forces have suffered tremendous losses, his economy is declining, and the democracies Putin sought to divide have united against him.

Alexander Motyl, political science professor at Rutgers University, points out that "the Russian performance has been undermined by Vladimir Putin's constant interference in military affairs. Inevitably, his inexperience and arrogance have resulted in a series of poor decisions."[16] Putin's view of himself as the hero has led to a top-down, command-and-control approach. Holed up and surrounded by "yes-men," Putin profoundly miscalculated Ukrainian resolve.

In addition to speeding decision-making and fostering creativity, decentralization develops leadership capabilities. When power is concentrated in the hands of a few, leadership skills become scarce. Decentralizing, however, requires employees to act as leaders in their local portion of the organization. With greater autonomy comes more decision-making, ownership, creativity, and intrapreneurship. The strength of the leadership bench increases dramatically.

Amy Hanlon-Rodemich, head of human resources at Nokia, believes strongly in the power of decentralization in big companies. She argues, however, that it takes time. At a previous company, she was able to decentralize much of the HR function, embedding HR capability in individual business units. That's because HR leaders in those units first agreed on simple rules for recruiting, onboarding, performance management, compensation, discipline, and other activities.

Other companies, by contrast, might be so fragmented—with people in different offices or regions acting quite differently—that leaders first need to centralize processes in order to standardize them. As the organization matures, and people develop a shared understanding of performance expectations, then headquarters can safely decentralize without fears of fragmentation. Employees in each business unit or region now have the relationships and shared understanding required to balance the needs of their local group with those of the broader enterprise. "It's sometimes a two-step process," Hanlon-Rodemich says. "You can't go from micromanaging to trusting everyone without first making sure everyone's on the same page."[17]

Overcoming Cultural Baggage

Some leaders have the added challenge of coming from a country that emphasizes hierarchical leadership. Arun was chief technology officer at a global financial services firm and an impressive engineer. He had immigrated from India, where he spent his early career working for the Indian government and later local technology companies. His talent ultimately led him to a senior position in the United States, but he was struggling to replicate the success he had previously enjoyed. His subordinates weren't following his orders and executing as he expected.

One of us (Dan) became his executive coach, and it soon became apparent that Arun felt pressure to be a hero rather than a community organizer. Given his previous experiences, this wasn't surprising. It turned out that the employees he had previously worked with most successfully were also immigrants from more hierarchical countries.

Geert Hofstede, a Dutch psychologist, captured this sense of hierarchy in the 1970s with the concept of power distance, the degree to which the disadvantaged members of a society accept and expect an unequal distribution of power. Turkey and Russia, along with India, score high on power distance, as did China even before Xi Jinping gained power. Austria, Israel, Denmark, New Zealand, and Ireland have the lowest power index scores, with the United States in the middle.[18]

Accordingly, leaders from more hierarchical cultures may be expected to command, control, reward, and punish their people, while employees from these cultures may be less likely to question commands and, fearing mistakes, expect clear instructions. As a result, leaders can slide into micromanagement, checking the execution of each command. This is exactly what was tripping up Arun.

Arun realized the cultural forces that were driving his behavior and creating blind spots. The insight helped him move away from heroism and toward facilitation. Although he still speaks directly with clear expectations and deliverables, he flexes his approach to be more inclusive and democratic.

Escaping the Trap

Everyone loves a hero—just look at Hollywood, a space dominated by superhero films. There's nothing more dramatic and exciting than someone swooping in to solve a problem stymying ordinary mortals. We all want to look up to heroes who make our lives better and require little of us.

But that's not how the world works (if it ever did). The villains aren't so clear or predictable, and it turns out even superheroes need those ordinary mortals to do most of the work.

It's time to see heroic intervention as a leadership trap, not a success. You'll be better off if you stay out of the limelight and quietly build up your teams to collectively handle challenges. Beyond curbing your own ego, you can decentralize, delegate, and broadly foster a sense of ownership that gets more done than you ever could.

7

Vive la Résistance!

After a successful stint as country manager for a global pharmaceutical company, Kesa had recently returned to the United
States to lead the company's US commercial operations. It was a sensitive time; 3,000 sales representatives had to learn a new approach
to engaging with prospects.

Pharmaceutical companies had always sought to convince doctors
to prescribe their drugs, but now that process had to change dramatically. In the past, they hired armies of outgoing, attractive sales reps
to deliver "core messages" to physicians. The reps were instructed to
repeat the drug's core message to a doctor multiple times in the same
conversation, often reading from a standardized visual aid. Questions
raised by a doctor were treated as "objections" to be overcome with
predefined, scripted responses. But new government guidelines and
the rise of managed care meant that sales reps couldn't simply meet
with doctors as before. And an increasingly diverse population and
the growth of specialty drugs left doctors with more questions
than ever.

Kesa's company had hired a consulting firm to develop a new sales
approach, one fitted to the new market conditions. Kesa liked the
approach and set out to find a region willing to pilot it. The reaction
disappointed her. Feedback ranged from "our sales reps don't have

the necessary capabilities" to "our existing systems won't support it" to "let's just tweak how we do it today." When Kesa shared the reaction with her boss, he replied with the established opinion, now a trap: "That's not surprising. People resist change. Figure out how to overcome it."

The Trap of Moving the Aircraft Carrier

Her boss's reaction is typical. The business environment is changing faster than ever, and companies must keep up. In the words of Jack Welch, former CEO of GE, "If the rate of change on the outside exceeds the rate of change on the inside, the end is near."[1] Companies must adapt or die.

Yet organizations are like aircraft carriers. They have a lot of inertia. Changing direction takes tremendous energy. What's more, unlike aircraft carriers, organizations are made up of people. You can't just turn a rudder. You must convince lots of different people, often in many different places and each with a point of view, to change how they work in a coordinated way. Common wisdom—"people are creatures of habit," "you can't teach an old dog new tricks"—tells us that getting people to change is difficult.

The point is hardly a new one. Five centuries ago, Machiavelli pointed out that "there is nothing more difficult to take in hand, more perilous to conduct, or more uncertain in its success, than to take the lead in the introduction of a new order of things. Because the innovator has for enemies all those who have done well under the old conditions, and lukewarm defenders in those who may do well under the new."[2]

Leaders often dismiss employees' negative responses as "resistance to change." In a world where organizations must continuously adapt, they see this resistance as a huge problem. Researchers agree. Some call it the biggest obstacle in an organization's efforts to improve and adapt. Others argue that the success of organizational transformation hinges on the perceptions and response of employees to change.

Experts recommend that leaders start by uncovering the root of this resistance in any given situation. Are employees resistant because they feel threatened by the unknown, a lack of control, the risk of failure, lost status or resources, or the disruption of their social relationships? Once leaders understand the resistance's source, they can choose an appropriate intervention, such as recruiting more senior leaders to publicly champion the change, communicating details about the change and its rationale, clarifying performance expectations, providing employees with training and resources, modifying reward systems, demonstrating and publicly recognizing quick wins, and enlisting managers and other internal influencers to act as change agents.

Notice that experts rarely advise leaders to treat resistance as information, or to work with the resisters on a better solution. Leaders just need to bring their people along. If that means steamrolling others, so be it. The idea that people resist change, and that leaders' job is to overcome this resistance, has become so well engrained in management thinking that leaders have come to expect it.

The Roots of Resistance

Despite the broad consensus that resistance hinders change and the many solutions proposed to address it, most organizational transformations still fail. Although experts report different numbers, most say that well over half of these efforts fall well short of expectations. One meta-analysis of change studies found only 40% of change initiatives had their intended impact.[3] Other researchers discovered that a third of significant, resource-intensive change efforts actually made things worse.[4] More recently, McKinsey & Co. suggested that 70% of change efforts fail, which they attributed, in large part, to employee resistance.[5]

All this failure is expensive. Ricardo Vargas, who directs the Project Management Institute's Brightline initiative, in 2018 tagged the cost of failed digital transformation efforts alone at $900 billion.[6] This expense doesn't include other types of unsuccessful transformation, nor does it consider the emotional toll on employees who have to deal with the disappointment of their failed efforts.

Could it be that our deep-rooted assumptions about employees' resistance to change are misguided? We say yes.

To understand how we got to this point, it's useful to examine where the notion of resistance, or inertia, originated. The initial idea dates back at least to Kepler, Galileo, and Newton, all of whom noted the tendency of a physical body to remain in a state of motion or rest until acted on by a force. Freud went on to apply the term to organic life, writing that there is an "inertia inherent in organic life: the human organism is inherently conservative and will change only when forced by external circumstances."[7]

Two decades later, in the 1930s, the pioneering psychologist Kurt Lewin introduced the concept of inertia to social systems. Lewin saw companies and other organizations as systems held in a dynamic balance between two sets of opposing forces: driving forces, which promote change, and restraining forces, which maintain the status quo. When the driving forces exceed resisting forces, they disrupt the organization's equilibrium, and change occurs. For Lewin, restraining forces were a system-level phenomena. They could come from outside the organization, emerging from market conditions, government regulations, social norms, or from inside the organization, from structures, policies and procedures, and employee beliefs.

Subsequent thinkers simplified Lewin's ideas. They focused on resistance from employees, leaving out the other restraining forces. In particular, they looked at employees' general state of mind, not on underlying reasons why employees might resist change. This move may have reflected the post-1930s growth of the labor movement in the United States, which led to sharp differentiations between labor and management. By focusing the idea of resistance to change on employees, managers could view themselves as the champions of organizational improvements and then blame employees if things didn't work out. Whatever the reason, the interpretation of resistance to change as we currently know it was solidified by the early 1960s and hasn't shifted much since.

Unfortunately, the simplified view of resistance to change has diminished leaders' ability to promote change, because it ignores the broader organization or system that Lewin described. Although disagreement or frustration on the part of employees can certainly constitute resistance, it's by no means the only source. What's more, as management expert John Kotter points out, individual resistance to change is actually rare. Kotter argues that resistance is much more likely to result from misalignment in the structure of the organization. Thus, when leaders spend time and energy on over-coming employees' resistance, they may well be focused on the wrong thing.

The conventional wisdom also assumes that leaders are the pro-ductive instigators of change, and that their job is to overcome employees' unproductive resistance. In fact, it's often senior leaders who resist change. In one study of 3,000 managers at Ford, middle managers blamed executives above them for resisting change.[8] This isn't surprising when you recognize, as Machiavelli did, that it's those in power who are typically most invested in maintaining the status quo.

Additionally, when leaders believe they must overcome resistance to change, they risk creating the very resistance they seek to sur-mount. After all, overcoming is about "getting the better of" some-thing or someone. It implies conflict between two opposing forces, with leaders heroically fighting for improvement and vanquishing resistance. They expect resistance and devise ways to defeat it. Others, less excited by conflict, may seek to disguise or hide the change. Either way, those affected by the change are likely to feel their concerns and ideas dismissed or ignored. Communication suffers and trust falls between leaders and employees. Resistance actually increases.

Perhaps the most pernicious aspect of the current view on resis-tance to change is that it devalues employee feedback. Leaders tend to label any pushback as resistance and feel justified dismissing it. The problem shifts from the change they're proposing to those who disagree with it.

Resistance Isn't Futile; It's Necessary

Dismissing employee feedback as resistance was less of an issue in stable environments. It gave leaders air cover to implement their plans without worrying about employees' feelings. After all, in stable environments, challenges were straightforward. Leaders, and their strategic planning departments, could rely on logic and intuition to determine the best course of action. Employees' role was to execute, not give advice. If leaders did get stuck, they could call in external experts to help figure things out. There were bound to be naysayers; there always are. Leaders simply needed to overcome this resistance and push forward.

That approach doesn't work in today's complex world, with business now involving too many interrelated and ever-changing forces. As we've seen, it's much harder to understand cause and effect or predict outcomes. When leaders treat employees' opposition as resistance, they miss out on critical insight and authentic information about what's happening on the front lines.

One enterprise we know fell into this trap. The company had been growing rapidly, but keeping up with customer demand left little time for building and aligning internal processes. As a result, each division had devised its own way of hiring, managing, and rewarding talent. By one count, the company had 12 different performance management systems. The lack of consistency made it hard to objectively compare talent across the enterprise or move people between groups. Engagement fell as employees realized that people were treated differently depending on where they worked in the company.

The head of HR operations, Lawrence, tried to install an enterprise-wide HR information system to standardize HR practices. It wasn't long before different groups raised concerns. The talent acquisition function objected to how the system would treat open job requisitions. They asked to delay the rollout, but Lawrence pushed ahead anyway. After all, some people were always going to resist. He had committed to a "go-live" date and wasn't going to miss it. Unfortunately, when the system did go live, many of the company's open job requisitions disappeared. Business leaders were furious about the subsequent delays in hiring. The talent acquisition team felt they had been disregarded and now needed to work overtime to solve the problem.

That resentment tends to spread. Dismissing employee feedback can dampen engagement broadly, as people learn that their opinions don't matter. By contrast, employees who believe their leaders encourage and are open to feedback are more likely to recommend their company as a great place to work. Engaged employees are safer, healthier, more loyal, and less likely to leave. They provide better customer service, improve quality, and generate higher productivity. There's no better way to kill that wonderful engagement than to force your "brilliant" plan and steamroll anyone in the way. Those who disagree are left humiliated and angry, while those who quietly go along feel disempowered.

Although our current understanding views resistance as problematic, the truth is just the opposite. Resistance is actually necessary for organizational health. In biology, most organisms work to maintain a stable internal environment despite changes in external conditions. For example, our bodies maintain a constant body temperature within a narrow range, sweating to cool off when it's hot or shivering to warm up in the cold. If our bodies didn't regulate our temperature, we'd be at continuous risk of heatstroke or hypothermia. Likewise, a degree of institutional resistance maintains the necessary stability, continuity, and legitimacy in organizations. Resistance to change is thus a form of organizational homeostasis.

The stability and predictability that resistance generates helps organizations consistently carry out complex tasks regardless of external pressures. Financial accounting standards, such as generally accepted accounting principles, serve as a homeostasis mechanism in organizations by providing a set of rules and guidelines for how financial information should be recorded and reported. These standards help to ensure that financial statements accurately reflect the financial position, performance, and cash flows of an organization. By adhering to these standards, organizations provide transparent and reliable financial information to investors, creditors, regulators, and other stakeholders. They maintain trust in companies generally and promote confidence in financial markets.

Of course, organizations, like organisms, must also adapt to external changes. The challenge for leaders, then, is not to overcome resistance but to balance stability and instability, control and freedom, the status quo and innovation.

Agile software development affords us one example of this equilibrium in practice. Originally designed for software development, Agile dispenses with detailed plans and rigid control systems. Instead, it promotes four core principles: individuals and interactions over processes and tools, working software over comprehensive documentation, customer collaboration over contract negotiation, and responding to change over following a plan.

Agile approaches might seem to embrace chaos, but they still involve governance and coordinating mechanisms with clear goals, defined roles and responsibilities, and regular communication among team members. The Agile manifesto explicitly recognizes the value of processes, documentation, and plans; it just values other things more. What matters is the ability to respond over time, rather than strictly follow plans set earlier.

This combination of stability and change is critical to successful adaptation. Stuart Kauffman, a theoretical biologist and complex systems researcher, found that systems that balance order and disorder are uniquely suited for adaptation and out-compete their peers. When systems emphasize order, they're rigid and can't adapt; but without some order, they descend into chaos. The sweet spot is a point between order and disorder, where the system's parts don't quite lock into place, and yet don't completely disintegrate either. This in-between space, which chaos theorist Norman Packard first referred to as the "edge of chaos," is where creativity flourishes.[9]

When organizations are poised between stability and disorder, their parts—employees, teams, and departments—interact in new ways. The recombination exposes everyone to different information, broadens their perspective, and opens new possibilities for action. The interactions between members create feedback loops that amplify what works and dampen what doesn't. Non-productive actions get crowded out, leading to recurring, collective behaviors. Thus, the organization evolves to a more productive state, a higher "fitness landscape."

In most complex systems, this evolution occurs without the intervention of a central controller. Change emerges bottom-up from the interaction of organizational members following simple rules. Like a school of fish, a financial market, or distributed computer network, the organization adapts and evolves in a self-organizing way. It gets what Kauffman calls *order for free*.[10]

Employees Own What They Cocreate

As an alternative to simply overpowering dissent, how can leaders create organizations that balance change and stasis? How can they implement systems or processes that engage employees themselves to help navigate change, unleashing employees' inherent dynamism and creativity rather than sparking a defensive response?

That starts, as we described in the previous chapter, with leaders relinquishing some control and the idea that they alone are responsible. Management philosopher Margaret Wheatley and coauthor point out that "Life always reacts to your directives; it never obeys them. It doesn't matter how visionary or strategic your message is. It can only elicit reactions, not straightforward compliance."[11]

That can be hard for leaders to accept. Most are comfortable in the driver's seat, with everyone else along for the ride. Many try to retain control while engaging others by soliciting feedback on their proposed change. Although this is beneficial, it doesn't generate the energy or motivation required to bring the change to life. It's one thing for employees to provide feedback on someone else's change. It's something else to be involved in building it. We've seen time and time again that people own what they co-create. They're far more likely to support and champion a change they had a hand in creating than one that was developed by someone else.

Asking for feedback also doesn't establish the relationships needed to execute. Organizational changes require new ways of working and interacting. When colleagues from across the enterprise collaborate to codesign a change, they start to form the connections necessary to implement it.

This doesn't mean that leaders need to give up complete control or stop planning. But it does mean their attention shifts. Instead of wrestling the organization into a new state of being, leaders become responsible for bringing together the right employees, setting direction, and establishing boundary conditions. The leader's job is to balance order and disorder at the edge of chaos.

Leaders can employ any of several whole-system approaches, such as Future Search, Search Conference, Work Out, and Open Space Technology. Each of these methods has two things in common. The first is that they bring together a group of people, typically with diverse expertise from across the enterprise, into the same physical or virtual space. Often, these individuals have not formally worked together before, which creates the disorder needed for adaptation. The second is providing the group with a collective purpose. This purpose typically involves a "far from equilibrium" condition, a significant threat or opportunity that the organization is unlikely to address in its existing form. The shared purpose creates structure by establishing a specific issue for the group to address. Because of its importance to the organization, the purpose boosts motivation and energy for group members to work together. It also increases similarity among group members; suddenly, they all have a common challenge, which helps to form new relationships.

This relationship rewiring is critical for adaptation. In a complex system, agents make decisions based only on the information available to them. Whether we're talking about a driver during rush hour or a bee looking for pollen, they act based on what they know. When we restructure the organization's informal network, the new connections between employees expose them to new information, from which they generate fresh insights and new solutions. Moreover, participants use their newly formed relationships for ongoing information sharing, problem-solving, and decision-making. This new relational infrastructure creates a scaffolding that can be used to operationalize what the group recommends.

Michael Arena, the former chief talent officer at General Motors and author of *Adaptive Space*, brought together dozens of younger, talented employees to spark creativity, develop new ways of working, and foster engagement at GM. At first, he got pushback. Higher-ups had trouble understanding how the initiative would create value for the company. They were used to top-down initiatives; a less-structured, employee-led approach felt very different. Arena spent considerable time with the executive sponsor going back and forth, tweaking the session's four business objectives and agenda, before he got approval for the event. Even then, the sponsor agreed only because he had already scheduled it.[12]

The session began with brief opening remarks from a high-level sponsor. The executive immediately left, but that was the senior-level endorsement and air cover Arena needed. Over the next two days the group toured startup environments in Detroit and worked together to flesh out innovative ways GM could operate. One group came up with a way of improving buyer-supplier relationships. Another group developed approaches for departments to work across silos to share problems. A snowstorm on the session's final day meant the session's main sponsor was freed up to attend the last hour and a half of the session. She was amazed by the level of interaction. When she stood up to close the session she shared: "I have to tell you I was completely wrong. This is exactly what we want to do in the organization. This is the level of energy we need. What do you need from me to support this?"

Interestingly, what came out of the session was very different from the four focus areas Arena had initially put forth. In total, participants came up with close to 30 different adaptive solutions. They formed groups for each one and continued to work on them long after the session was over. According to Arena, "We never would have come up with as many brilliant ideas if we'd done it top-down. Most importantly, the groups' feeling of ownership meant many of the solutions came to fruition. Some had just two people working on them, others had as many as 15. Many were still going strong 18 months later."

For this to work, however, leaders must choose participants wisely. If the group members already work together closely, they are likely to be connected and share the same information. Instead, leaders need to include people with limited exposure to one another and who bring diverse expertise and points of view related to the group's intended purpose. The greater diversity of thought, the deeper the group's understanding of the issue, and the more insight it has with which to develop creative solutions.

Arena recalls another example where he brought together young employees and senior leaders to help launch a change initiative at GM. What the group quickly realized, however, is that they were missing a critical stakeholder group: middle managers. When it was mentioned, the room got quiet. Middle managers were perceived as champions of the status quo and slow to change. Then someone suggested, "What if we decide which ones to invite?" Arena asked, "How will you decide?" And someone else said, "Let's pick the ones that are fun to play with." Looking back, Arena says the 20 middle managers selected by the team made all the difference. They became the catalyst for the change and were responsible for getting other middle managers committed to the program.[13]

Besides defining a shared purpose for the group, leaders must dictate the relevant boundary conditions. These constraints come in three forms.[14] Input constraints, such as budget, time, or human capital, limit the resources that groups have at their disposal. Process constraints specify a methodology or approach, such as design thinking, that groups should apply to carry out their work. Finally, output constraints require that the group's results meet certain requirements. For example, the leader might stipulate that the solution the group defines cannot change the organization's formal reporting structure.

Specifying conditions makes sure that the group doesn't operate outside the bounds of what's acceptable. This is important because groups may otherwise waste energy on and become invested in untenable courses of action. It's much better to tell group members what's off the table at the start rather than after they've become excited about an idea. Constraints combined with freedom actually spur creativity and innovation by preventing complacency. Instead of latching on to the first idea that comes to mind, groups invest in developing better ideas. Constraints provide focus and motivate people to search for and connect information from different sources to generate novel ideas.

Leaders must be careful, however, not to impose many conditions, because these can sap the group's motivation and minimize members' freedom to explore. In general, the greater the change needed, the fewer constraints leaders should impose. The increased flexibility enables groups to explore further afield to discover novel and compelling solutions.

Leaders must also promote psychological safety among the group. Not having worked together in the past, group members may hesitate to share ideas or ask questions for fear of looking foolish. This can undermine the exchange of information and creativity. Leaders accelerate participants' comfort by creating psychological safety, the shared belief that no one will be penalized for speaking up with ideas, questions, or concerns. Leaders increase psychological safety by acknowledging that the path forward is uncertain, that it's only by testing several ideas that don't work that the group will find the one that does, that mistakes are expected and part of the process, and that everyone needs to contribute for the group to succeed. Leaders can also model curiosity. When leaders like David Chang, at WuXi AppTec (see Chapter 3), admit they don't know the answer and ask others to share their insights, they create psychological safety by showing that it's okay to be fallible.

To sum up, when a leader brings together a diverse group of experts who haven't worked together before, focuses the group on a shared purpose, establishes boundary conditions, and builds psychological safety, they create the ideal conditions for adaptation. The group is positioned between order and disorder; they're poised at the edge of chaos. The new connections that are formed not only generate new solutions but also the pathways to execute them.

Leaders may feel that this is a lot to ask to get only a small group of people to change. But as complexity researchers emphasize, the whole is greater than the sum of its parts. Just as those 20 GM middle managers drove change across the enterprise, a group's efforts often extend far beyond its initial membership. Organizations don't change one person at a time. *Organizations change as networks of relationships form among people united by a common purpose and vision.*

The resolution to Kesa's story from the beginning of this chapter follows a similar pattern. Kesa wasn't so sure about her boss' guidance to simply compel people to adopt the new sales model. So instead, she invited 70 people to the company's US headquarters to work on the challenge. Participants included sales reps, marketers, trainers, executives, individuals from third-party agencies, and a handful of external physicians.

As Kesa recalls, "We came up with an approach where the sales rep doesn't tell the doctor what to think, but instead starts by understanding what's important to the doctor. We switched it from a monologue to a dialogue. It wasn't that different from what the consulting firm recommended, but it was a lot more detailed and fleshed out." When Kesa asked who would be willing to pilot the approach, she was inundated. The pilot quickly became 80% of the entire US sales force. And, because of its success, two years later the approach was rolled out globally—far more broadly than originally intended. According to Kesa, "If we'd just steamrolled everyone, the initial approach wouldn't have had the same effect. People needed to feel like they had a hand in creating it to really get behind it."

Escaping the Trap

Leaders do sometimes need to overpower resistance to change. Employees may in fact be resistant due to short-sightedness or a self-interested fear of losing one's position. But this resistance is less common than leaders assume. When leaders fixate on employee resistance, they gratify their egos but risk missing the big picture by implementing suboptimal solutions that generate further resistance—digging them deeper in the hole.

Especially in unpredictable markets, leaders need to shift their focus from overcoming resistance toward acting as a catalyst. They need to dedicate themselves to creating conditions from which the organization itself evolves in response to emerging conditions. Effective leaders apply principles of complex adaptive systems, balancing order and disorder. Poised at the edge of chaos, employees consider new possibilities, develop breakthrough solutions, and form the relationships needed to bring them to life.

8

Resilience Beats Efficiency

In 2008, when Toyota became the world's largest automaker, few saw how the source of this growth would come back to haunt the company. Much of the company's success stemmed from the Toyota Production System, better known as lean manufacturing. Focused on eliminating the seven sources of waste—overproduction, inventory, excess motion, defects, overprocessing, waiting, and excess transport—lean manufacturing has been copied by manufacturers all around the world.

Although lean manufacturing is highly efficient and profitable, it also introduces fragility into companies. A single failure can disrupt an entire supply chain, halting global operations. That's what happened at Toyota in March 2011, when a 9.0 magnitude earthquake struck Japan, causing a series of tsunamis that devastated the country's east coast. In a matter of hours, the company lost much of its supply base. The damage hit factories that made over a thousand parts for three-quarters of the company's vehicles. Quarterly profits fell more than 75%.

In the short term, the company focused on protecting human life, aiding rapid recovery of disaster areas, and resuming production. But afterward, Toyota reviewed all its suppliers, even the most indirect, to understand how it could better balance efficiency with resilience. It decided to pull back on lean manufacturing in order to reduce its vulnerability and boost its safety margins It realized that efficiency isn't everything—that a little "waste" wasn't so bad after all.

The Trap of Efficiency

As its name suggests, economics is the science of economizing, of optimizing the use of scarce resources, of doing more with less. In *The Wealth of Nations* (1776), Adam Smith explained that specialization through the division of labor would make a commercial enterprise vastly more efficient. David Ricardo in "The Principles of Political Economy and Taxation" (1817) added his theory of comparative advantage, suggesting it's more efficient for the Portuguese to focus on winemaking and the English on clothmaking, leading to greater benefits for both. The 20th century developers of systematic management took these insights further, leading to W. Edwards Deming's Total Quality Management system, out of which Toyota developed lean manufacturing.

From Henry Ford's decision to produce the Model T only in black to today's platform strategies, outsourcing, and automation, companies have devoted enormous effort to reducing time, materials, and capital. This effort goes by many names, such as cost reduction, restructuring, process re-engineering, and profit maximization. Even efforts at growth, which bring learning and scale efficiencies, often serve to boost efficiency and optimize resource use.

The aggressive pursuit of efficiency makes sense in stable environments where leaders understand cause and effect and can optimize how their organization works accordingly. Efficiency has benefited many businesses beyond Toyota, generating tremendous wealth for owners. And the returns to society can't be overstated. Over the last two centuries, life expectancy, education, and living standards have all risen around the world. Before then, most people presumed that poverty was the norm and that only a tiny percentage of society could be wealthy.

In unstable environments, however, emphasizing efficiency brings substantial new costs, starting with fragility. Small, unforeseen complications or hiccups can break an entire operation, damaging not just individual organizations but society as a whole. As described by Roger Martin, a strategy advisor and former business school dean, "an excessive focus on efficiency can produce startlingly negative effects, to the extent that superefficient businesses create the potential for social disorder."[1]

Many people think of companies as falling along a normal distribution or bell curve. They imagine that a small number of companies in an industry are highly efficient and make a lot of money; most firms are relatively efficient and make less money; and the remainder are inefficient, make little money, and are at risk of failing. As companies work hard to become more efficient or make missteps and become less efficient, they move left or right on the bell curve relative to competitors, reaping the associated rewards or consequences.

Yet "normal distribution" doesn't actually apply to company profits and market share. These phenomena tend toward a Pareto distribution, or the 80–20 rule. The vast majority of profits and market share in an industry typically go to a small number of firms. Their greater scale in turn enables them to lower costs and further distance themselves from would-be competitors. Hence, the rich get richer.

As it turns out, this process is accelerated in complex environments characterized by stress and interconnectivity. As the business environment becomes more connected through technologies such as the Internet of Things, Pareto effects may well accelerate.[2]

We've watched this trend unfold in recent years. Since 1990, 75% of industries in the United States have become more consolidated.[3] Additionally, wealth inequality has grown steadily with the top 1% now owning a third of the nation's wealth. Thomas Piketty, author of *Capital in the Twenty-first Century*, describes the long-term effects as "potentially terrifying."[4]

With these winner-take-all realities in mind, companies often prioritize efficiency over other goals, a tendency that the decades-long emphasis on shareholder returns only enhances. This priority on efficiency is apparent in the decision to not equip the Texas power grid with common weatherproofing features that could have prevented the deaths of 200 people during winter storm Uri in 2021. Despite repeated recommendations from the state's utility commission, the service provider emphasized returns over reliability.[5]

In addition to making companies more vulnerable to natural disasters, the relentless pursuit of efficiency can also produce choke points that lead to catastrophic failure. Many companies now outsource critical tasks to less-expensive suppliers. As these suppliers scale their operations, they further reduce their costs, attracting even more customers. Over time they become the dominant supplier and now exert leverage over those customers.

For example, in an effort to reduce costs, many drug companies outsourced manufacturing to China, now the world's largest producer of active pharmaceutical ingredients. COVID-19 and trade disputes, however, have disrupted imports of at least one drug to the United States. The situation is severe enough that the Pentagon has called the US dependence on China for medication a national security challenge.[6]

An excessive emphasis on efficiency isn't just a macro-level issue. It has direct implications for leaders of individual enterprises who inadvertently make their companies vulnerable to unforeseen failures. Consider Boeing's 737 Max. In designing the aircraft, Boeing retrofitted the earlier 737 design with more efficient engines. That reduced costs and accelerated the planes' availability, but also caused flight instability, which a new flight-control algorithm was intended to correct. The algorithm, however, relied on information from a single sensor. If that single sensor failed, software assumed the aircraft was stalling and automatically put it into a dive to recover from a stall that wasn't, in fact, occurring. The unanticipated failure caused two terrible crashes and forced Boeing to ground hundreds of aircraft for nearly two years.

Unanticipated failures will continue to happen. We don't know what they will be or when they will occur, but they are inevitable. Researchers have studied catastrophic failures since at least the Three Mile Island nuclear accident. In *Normal Accidents*, Charles

Perrow determined that in environments with high complexity and interconnectedness—our current business context—failures are unavoidable. They cannot be prevented, but can be mitigated by balancing efficiency with resilience.[7] Otherwise, the relentless pursuit of lower costs leaves companies vulnerable.

How Resilience Creates Competitive Advantage

If efficiency is about optimizing for current conditions, resilience is about optimizing for potential *future* conditions. In stable environments, when circumstances are slow to change, efficiency and resilience are largely synonymous. Indeed, many traditional theories of economics assume the future will look like the present. However, this is no longer the case. Business school professors Gary Hamel and Liisa Valikangas point out that "every business is successful until it's not. What's amazing is how often top management is surprised when 'not' happens."[8]

Simply put, resilience is the ability to recover when the "not" happens—to bounce back after disruption. Firms with greater resilience anticipate crises, cope with the corresponding stress, restore critical functionality, and take advantage of the altered circumstances. In our current era of complexity, efficiency provides a short-term competitive edge while resilience offers a sustainable competitive advantage.

Research increasingly shows that resilient organizations outperform their peers in the face of adversity. When the Boston Consulting Group analyzed 1,800 US companies from 1995 to 2020, they found resilience was a critical predictor of performance over time.[9] Companies that outperformed their peers during a crisis were twice as likely to outperform over the long run. Moreover, the more impactful the crisis, the greater the value of resilience.

Some firms try to see and interpret early warning signs in their environment. They can't prevent every crisis, but they can prepare sooner than others. A study of the roughly 100 major US companies with earnings calls between January 24 and February 24, 2020, when the coronavirus pandemic was only starting to expand beyond China, found only 10 discussed the possibility of a global pandemic affecting their business. Seven of those firms outperformed their industry peers when the pandemic eventually spread.[10]

In addition to spotting threats sooner, resilient companies can absorb a disruption's initial shock and recover faster. That's partly because these companies are more likely to rapidly accept the situation, rather than denying a looming disaster or taking a wait-and-see attitude. They tend to be better at integrating expertise and experience to improvise creative solutions and then rapidly transfer resources to execute faster.

Moreover, resilience isn't just about keeping the company going after suffering a heavy blow. As Nassim Nicholas Taleb describes in *Antifragile*, it's about coming back stronger. Resilient companies systematically change how they work in response to disruptions. They "never let a good crisis go to waste." After the 2011 earthquake, Toyota broadened its supply chain, reducing efficiency but bolstering resilience.

Similarly, volatile environments can bring growth as well as decline. When the Great Recession hit in 2008 one financial services firm saw its revenues plummet. Concerned about the company's survival, the board urged the CEO to cut a third of all employees. Yet the CEO believed the turmoil would ultimately create a new set of opportunities. Worried he wouldn't be able to restaff in time, he pushed back on his directors. Instead of cutting staff across the board, he cut some administrative positions but fought to maintain the company's highly knowledgeable field staff members, necessary for reengaging customers as demand returned, and to increase R&D investments. The bet paid off with substantial growth after the crisis.

Although resilience is immensely valuable, building it requires a difficult trade-off. For centuries, leaders have emphasized efficiency. That's often how they rose in the hierarchy. Championing resilience means adopting a new mindset as well as modifying the structures and incentives that support the status quo.

What's more, companies' emphasis on short-term results means that resilience often appears less rewarding than efficiency. The benefits of resilience often come only with a crisis, and although crises are increasing, they are still infrequent enough that many leaders and inventors can ignore them. As Moshe Vardi, a computational engineering professor at Rice University, has pointed out, people and markets are bad at preparing for low-probability events. Otherwise, governments wouldn't have to force people to buy car insurance.

Gains in resilience are also much harder to measure than increases in efficiency. Most financial accounting systems focus on revenues and costs. It's hard for leaders to assess their organization's current fragility, justify investments in resilience, or measure progress over time.

Efficiency also flows naturally from many leaders' quest for perfection and control. Yet perfection is a resource-intensive pursuit, and anything that's perfect today is likely to be suboptimal when things change, which they will. The only way to thrive in unstable times is to embrace vulnerability (discussed in Chapter 3) and uncertainty (addressed in Chapter 11). This change in thinking, however, can be difficult for leaders to adopt, many of whom are most comfortable exhibiting certainty and confidence.

Of course, a singular emphasis on resilience at the expense of efficiency isn't desirable either. Resilience and efficiency are both vital to long-term success. The job of leaders is to balance the two. That's what the US Aviation Administration does in managing air traffic control at the major airports. Instead of pursuing lean staffing, leaders there talk about the "safety envelope," enough redundancy to maintain continual operation and prevent accidents and burnout, while not so much that air travel becomes unaffordable.

Pinpointing Weak Signals

The good news is that leaders can make adjustments to increase resilience while still maintaining some degree of efficiency. One way to do so is by thinking longer term and developing greater foresight. The US Office of Technology Assessment (OTA) was a congressional agency charged with helping the Congress develop public policy related to technology. It operated from 1974 to 1995, and one of us (Steve) worked there in the early 1990s. The thinking was that members of Congress and their staffs might lack the technical expertise to grasp the breadth of issues on new and expanding technologies. Instead of turning to lobbyists for answers, lawmakers could ask a team of nonpartisan researchers and scientists at OTA. For more than 20 years, the office produced studies related to everything from aging to telecommunications. In one prescient report, OTA warned that private electronic data collected from computer systems could undermine citizens' constitutional rights.

In 1995 a new Congress, which had promised to shrink government and end wasteful spending, defunded OTA. At the time, a Republican representative, Amo Houghton, criticized the decision, saying, "we are cutting off one of the most important arms of Congress when we cut off unbiased knowledge about science and technology."[11] Although the move boosted governmental efficiency by cutting costs, we can only wonder how OTA might have contributed to a better understanding of today's many complex and controversial technologies, such as generative AI or gene editing.

Leaders can gain a similar kind of foresight in their organizations by assembling a cross-disciplinary group of experts charged with assuming a dynamic and systemic view of the organization and its environment. Such a group challenges reigning assumptions and explores the range of possibilities and conditions under which they might occur. Unlike strategic planning, focused on setting goals and determining the most efficient path to achieve them, or risk management, which addresses a few well-defined potential calamities, a resilience advisory group asks about future contingencies generally: under what conditions might business disruption occur, what are the potential ramifications, and how might we better prepare for them?

One way these groups generate foresight is by looking for "weak signals" in the external environment. In the words of cyberpunk pioneer William Gibson, "The future is already here; it's just not evenly distributed yet."[12] The trick is to spot this future from weak signals— data points suggesting a significant change is under way. Weak signals come in many forms. Futurist Amy Webb suggests looking for contractions (when events occur in a manner opposite of the expected), hacks (products or services used in unintended ways), inflections (sudden bursts of activity or capital investments), and extremes (when ideas, services, or technologies are pushed beyond established boundaries to create something new).

The detection of a weak signal caused Dr. Leonard S. Schleifer, CEO at drug company Regeneron, to focus on COVID. He was watching the news when he learned that the Chinese were constructing a colossal new hospital in Wuhan. "They said they were going to build a hospital in five days. I said to myself, 'Holy cow, OK, this doesn't happen just for the fun of it.'"[13] Regeneron expanded their partnership with the federal government and accelerated the manufacture of antibodies, which resulted in one of the first effective treatments for COVID.

The Firebreak Approach

A more straightforward way to build resilience is through redundancy. Amazon Web Services (AWS), the world's largest cloud-computing provider, keeps costs low but knows a thing or two about resilience. Over a million businesses rely on AWS services. When AWS services go down, those businesses and their customers feel the pain. To ensure resilience, AWS has established a highly redundant network architecture. Each AWS region includes multiple availability zones, or data centers. If one availability zone fails, a different zone in the same region can quickly assume its workload.

Redundancy alone is not sufficient—companies need to investigate how and where those backup resources work. Several financial institutions on Wall Street sought to build resilient communication systems by relying on multiple telecommunications providers. As it turned out, those providers' cables all ran under the World Trade Center. When the Twin Towers collapsed on September 11, 2001, the financial institution's communications all failed.

To create true redundancy, companies must segment or decouple those multiple sources. AWS, for example, isolates its availability zones, placing them in different buildings with separate power, cooling, and networking. Likewise Google relies on a zero-trust approach to cybersecurity. It requires all users, both inside and outside the company, to be authenticated and continuously validated. Although less efficient than simply assuming anyone within Google's network is friendly, this system is more secure and therefore more resilient.

Similar to firebreaks that stop advancing wildfires or social distancing that reduces the risk of infection, Amazon's availability zoning and Google's zero-trust approach compartmentalize possible disruptions. These policies build resilience by reducing the risk of a single failure spreading broadly.

Leaders in any business can do the same by answering a few simple questions. What functionality is mission critical? How can we replicate it cost-effectively? And how can we ensure the replicated instances are separated and not co-dependent?

In answering these questions after the 2011 earthquake, Toyota put in place a 60/20/20 model that divided spending among multiple suppliers. In case of problems at the primary supplier, the one providing 60% of the volume, the other two suppliers could increase production to fill the deficit. The shift helped Toyota maintain full production longer than its rivals did, when the 2020–2022 pandemic disrupted supplies of semiconductor chips and other vital supplies.

Cushioning the Inevitable Blows

As a complement to redundancy, buffering minimizes disruption by insulating a company against shocks. To prepare for a likely recession that raises capital costs, many companies stockpile cash. The US government maintains the Strategic Oil Reserve, an emergency stockpile of petroleum, to mitigate supply shocks such as an OPEC embargo. In the wake of the COVID-19 pandemic and its supply chain disruptions, manufacturers, such as Toyota, are tamping down their enthusiasm for just-in-time inventory by increasing lead times and building up reserves of spare parts.

Organizations can also buffer their most important asset: their people. This is particularly important because, as the US Securities & Exchange Commission learned from analysis of the September 11 attacks, people are critical to keeping institutions functioning in times of crisis.[14] Yet although many leaders talk about the importance of human capital, few do much to buffer employees. If anything, many companies are doubling down on employee efficiency by treating labor as an expense to minimize.

More than half of all mid-size and large US companies now use corporate surveillance technologies to record the keystrokes of employees. It's unclear how many use the programs aggressively, to monitor "productivity," but relying on any surveillance shows the extent of a concern for efficiency. Applying the software sends a chilling message to employees: focus on your prescribed immediate task and don't explore possibilities that might help the company but run afoul of productivity guidelines.

Creativity often requires stepping back from the task at hand. Researchers call this *the shower effect*, when minds wander while engaged in rote activities such as showering or walking.[15] It's exactly this creativity that's needed during disruption when employees must figure out how to solve problems that have never been seen before. A heavy emphasis on employee efficiency winds up exacting a hidden toll on companies, rendering them less resilient

A subset of companies do proactively buffer their human capital. Some, such as 3M, have historically set aside a percentage of employees' time to innovate and learn. We have this innovation–time-off strategy to thank for the creation of Post-it Notes and Google News. In another approach, some companies are adopting a four-day work week. In one of the largest studies to date, a six-month pilot including 70 companies in Britain, initial feedback suggests no loss in employee productivity.[16] Besides creating slack that companies can draw on during a crisis, the program appears to boost innovation and employee well-being.

Buffering human capital isn't just about reserving a portion of people's time. By increasing their engagement and improving capabilities, the policy encourages employees to apply more discretionary effort in a pinch. When Ben Fried became CIO at Google, one of his first decisions was determining which laptops most employees should use. Because the company creates software, information technology is a large cost center. The typical approach would be to identify a single manufacturer and select a few laptop options to keep costs low. But Fried had seen how cheap laptops discouraged talented employees. Some had even resorted to using their personal machines.

The choice was also a matter of self-image. Many Google developers prided themselves on their coding skills. Fried wanted their tools to reflect how they viewed themselves, as craftspeople, and to equip them to address whatever challenge presented itself. He dramatically expanded employees' choices of laptops. Fried even arranged with the (multiple) vendors to send each machine directly to employees, so they could open it fresh out of the box.

Fried took a similar approach with technical support. He ended the commonplace practice of outsourcing and the reliance on scripts to handle most problems. Google's employees were smart people who knew their way around computers; why subject them to people who probably understood laptops less than they did? Accordingly, he brought the help desk in-house as part of the main IT structure and made them "advisors" on a career track to rise into the main engineering organization. They dropped the scripts and started talking to employees as colleagues. Their main metric became time to repair or resolve, not "productivity," because the company's business model depended on expensive engineering talent working steadily.

On the face of it, both changes were absurdly inefficient. But Fried wasn't optimizing for the cost of IT. He was optimizing for Google's long-term success, especially in its highly dynamic industry. More engaged employees meant more capacity and greater resilience in a crisis.

Building Resilience Through Variety

Yet another way leaders can build resilience is by pursuing diversity. Just as forests with a greater variety of species can better resist drought, disease, and predators, diverse organizations are better at dealing with turbulence. As Gary Hamel points out, "Resilience depends on variety."[17]

Diversity, in contrast to standardization, fosters resilience in several ways. Organizations whose workforces have diverse backgrounds, experiences, and expertise (including but beyond the usual criteria of demographic diversity) bring a broader and richer knowledge base to challenging times. They can use this knowledge to detect and decode signals from the external environment as well as to devise innovative solutions to emerging problems.

Leaders can learn from the playbook of US President Franklin D. Roosevelt, who took the redundancy idea a step further. Roosevelt won election on a promise to avoid deficit spending, but in March 1933 the economic hardship had deepened to the point of social breakdown. Roosevelt didn't have a solution, so he asked separate aides to work up potential plans. Most of them didn't even know they were working on the same problem, but the different perspectives generated creative solutions, such as strengthening workers and consumers, that led to better results over time.

Amazon has followed such a multipath approach for decades with its "two is better than none" operating principle. No one can fault the company for ignoring efficiency—it famously keeps its prices low and forces the organization to find savings in unexpected places. But speed matters even more as the company pursues its overall strategy of using technology to improve consumer shopping.

Amazon was already developing autonomous robots that could lift and transport carts from one part of a warehouse to another, but it acquired Canvas Technology in 2019 because the Canvas engineers tackled the same problem differently. Instead of building autonomous robots that could carry carts, Canvas was automating the carts themselves. The acquisition enabled Amazon to experiment with two approaches simultaneously to see which worked for its specific use cases. Once it determined what worked best, it transferred all the associated resources to the winning team.

By tolerating redundancy upfront, Amazon found a better mix of solutions. But that's the mindset of leaders of an agile, emergent organization: we don't know what will work best in the real world, so let's test different approaches to find out.

Leaders can also diversify their organization's broader business models. When he was CEO at Microsoft, Bill Gates is reported to have said that the company was always two or three years away from failure. True or not, the message was clear: the company needed to continually reinvent itself. And Microsoft certainly has reinvented itself since the mid-2010s. It shifted from being a Windows-reliant, PC-based provider to one with multiple platforms on the web as well as significant investments in generative AI.

Leaders that put all their eggs in one basket risk losing everything if the basket fails. Better to diversify the employee base to bring in new perspectives, and diversify the business portfolio by distributing time and resources across products, channels, geography, and business models.

Collaboration as Readiness

Cross-enterprise collaboration also boosts resilience, because it enables leaders to quickly draw resources from across the organization. When someone collapses from a heart attack, clear coordination is vital. The Red Cross advises CPR trainees to point at specific onlookers and issue direct commands: "You, call 911! You, go get a defibrillator!" This makes sure everyone knows what to do and that vital tasks don't fall through the cracks in an emergency.

Complex, unprecedented crises, of course, have no preestablished protocol. Multiple people must craft solutions, drawing on their individual expertise. They must then work in concert to generate and test new ideas. The individuals involved may not have worked together; they never had a need before. So people must be ready to collaborate across traditional reporting lines.

Leaders can help to build this readiness through interventions such as cross-functional mentoring, peer-learning circles, and networking software. These efforts are as much about building trust for future collaboration as for addressing a near-term, explicit goal. Leaders who focus on the task at hand, taking no time to socialize, may think they're being efficient, but they don't build the relationships they need when things go wrong.

Ginger Miller, who started her career as a labor delivery nurse, is now the chief operating officer at the benefit plan administrator WPAS. Miller remembers urgently needing information from one of her directors to respond to a client. When she went to get the information, however, she found the director visibly upset over an exchange with one of the company's account executives.[18]

Rather than press for her information on the spot, Miller spent an hour listening to and helping the director think about how she could handle the situation. A few hours later Miller came back to get what she needed. Miller recalls, "My experience as a nurse has taught me you need to meet people where they are. You never know what you're going to find when you walk into a patient's room and you have to adjust. If I'd ignored how upset she was and just pushed her for the information she might have just shut down. Sometimes, you have to go slow to go fast." Ultimately, Miller's client got the information in time and Miller deepened the relationship with her colleague.

Taken too far, however, collaboration can actually undermine resilience. Rob Cross, professor of global leadership at Babson College, found that over the past decade, the amount of time employees spend communicating with others by email, instant messaging, and video conferences has increased by 50%, and now consumes 85% of knowledge workers' time.[19] Cross points out that these employees risk *collaboration overload*, which can slow decisions and reduce productivity, not to mention undermine organizational resilience. Excessive inclusion saps the organization's human capital buffers.

If people burn out from nonstop meetings and email exchanges, it's hard to rouse them to collaborate in a crisis.

Tap External Networks for Hidden Reserves

What about drawing on support from the company's external economic or social system? Some companies do that by leaning on their communities, customers, and suppliers at difficult times. At such "embedded" companies, close connections to the company's broader ecosystem can motivate employees as well as offer protection and adaptability. We saw the value of embeddedness vividly in the experiences of small businesses during the COVID-19 pandemic. On the verge of failure, many reached out to local communities and received outpourings of support that helped them survive.

Businesses can increase embeddedness by deepening their relationship with external stakeholders. When David Cote was CEO of Honeywell, he made a point of prepaying suppliers for parts during downtimes. The strategy not only helped his suppliers but ensured he got first dibs on critical parts when the economy bounced back. Cote credits the approach with helping two of Honeywell's businesses, aerospace and controls, outpace competitors. In a less common but still relevant example of embeddedness, Elon Musk asked Twitter users to vote on whether or not he should remain as the company's CEO. Having helped make the governance decision, Twitter's users are more likely to stay on the platform in the future.

Escaping the Trap

Leaders have long been encouraged to increase efficiency and eliminate redundancy. But in turbulent markets, a singular focus on efficiency becomes a trap. The most efficient organizations are so optimized for their current environment that they lack the capacity or slack to cushion against unexpected or disruptive environments. In slow-moving environments this was seldom an issue. In today's rapidly changing world, however, efficiency can lead to fragility.

Alternatively, leaders must balance efficiency and resiliency. The challenge is that efficiency is easy to measure and wins immediate praise from the bean counters, while resilience is hard to quantify. Strong leaders in volatile, unpredictable markets need to resist the temptation to focus on efficiency. They can do that by investing in foresight, redundancy, buffering, diversity, and collaboration.

This is not a call to go back to the 1960s, when big companies built extensive, and expensive, corporate structures and tried to control much of their activities in-house. Successful companies still need to outsource work to specialists, and they still need to offer affordable products. Leaders must balance resilience and efficiency. But that work starts by recognizing the pervasive pressure for efficiency and by regularly assessing the external environment to see what's changing—noting especially the contraindications, hacks, and other extreme or rare developments.

From there, leaders can devise experiments to exploit these oddities, with the assumption that most trials will fail. All of these efforts will inform this ongoing balancing act between efficiency and resilience. Leaders can also take the long view by exploring various scenarios of disruption, examining what they might do now to position the company for success or at least survival.

9

The Siren Song of Certainty

George had set himself up for a fall. He was the newly promoted chief strategy officer for a $4 billion global financial technology company. A brilliant analyst, his well-earned reputation as the smartest person at the table had powered him up the corporate ladder. But having reached the C-suite, George now felt pressure to justify his position. He knew that the CEO, Jack, admired self-confidence and strong conviction in his leaders, and George made a point of displaying those qualities to remain in Jack's good graces.

As part of an ambitious strategy to reach $7 billion in revenue in two years, George placed nine-figure bets on acquisitions in 2019. He expected one key addition, based in Shanghai, to open a $3 billion–plus market for the company's products. Based on what had worked in the firm's previous expansion in South Korea, he was certain of how the newly acquired firm should approach the major financial institutions in China.

The first six months didn't go as planned. The newly acquired operation struggled to gain traction, and its leaders were reluctant to enact some of George's recommendations. George attributed the difficulty to the competence of those local leaders, not to the strategy he had assuredly pushed. He raised his concerns and strongly encouraged the executive who oversaw Asia to replace members of the team. When Jack questioned George on these matters, George insisted that his analysis and strategic approach were correct, and that the company should stay the course.

But when the situation further deteriorated, George decided to fly to Shanghai to meet in person with the local leadership team. Together they undertook a fact-finding exercise, making sure everyone was operating from the same information and was transparent about their assumptions and analysis. Through the conversations, George learned about several downstream implications and potential unintended consequences of his strategy.

Both he and the local leaders came to better understand the firm's needs, constraints, and changing conditions in the target market. George realized that his approach did indeed require a critical pivot. Now aligned with the local leadership team, he returned to New York and, somewhat sheepishly, explained to Jack the need to change course. But improved results over the next six months proved that the pivot was a valuable move. By letting go of his posture of certainty, George opened himself to new information that helped the company adapt in a crucial way.

The Certainty Trap

Leaders, like everyone else, crave certainty. It provides a sense of security, stability, and control—they feel that they know what to expect and what is expected of them. It makes them less anxious as they make decisions and plan.

Certainty is actually a basic human desire; what psychologists call the *need for closure*. This need can lead people to embrace the first definite answer they encounter and subsequently wall themselves off from additional information to minimize the risk of disruptions. They narrowly define their reality to what they can control in order to make the situation manageable. In the words of Sherlock Holmes, the second greatest fictional detective, "Any truth is better than indefinite doubt."[1]

Certainty is also simply less work. Daniel Kahneman, Nobel Prize–winning psychologist and economist, distinguishes between two modes of thinking. System 1 is the fast, automatic system that operates largely outside our awareness. Highly efficient, it's responsible for quick judgments and decisions in response to environmental stimuli. System 2 is our deliberate, slow, conscious mode of thinking responsible for complex problem-solving and decision-making. According to Mark Schaefer, author of *The Certainty of Uncertainty*, System 2 "requires a great deal more processing power and energy. . . In short, certainty is easier on the brain than uncertainty is; uncertainty requires more mental effort."[2]

Historically, seeking certainty made sense. The market was less complex, and leaders could figure out causes and effects and predict outcomes over time, allowing them to confidently forecast into the future. By contrast, in today's turbulent business climate, new threats and opportunities can appear overnight. When ChatGPT launched in November 2022, it reached a million subscribers in five days. Educators scrambled to figure out how to prevent their students from using it to cheat, and Google issued an emergency "Code Red" to thwart the algorithm's potential to upend its $150 billion search business.

In this disruptive context, a posture of certainty is no longer an asset, it's a trap. It causes leaders to lock in on preconceived notions that may well turn out to be wrong as the market shifts unexpectedly. When Apple launched the iPhone in 2007, Microsoft, which was pursuing its own mobile strategy, wasn't worried. CEO Steve Ballmer reacted by saying, "That is the most expensive phone in the world. And it doesn't appeal to business customers because it doesn't have a keyboard."[3] What Microsoft missed was that for many people, an internet-connect phone would replace the personal computer. Ballmer's certainty helps explain Microsoft's failure in the mobile market. Three years after the iPhone's launch, Apple surpassed Microsoft to become the world's most valuable technology company.

Certainty also stifles creativity. It leads us to stick to what we know, and to value established ideas over new approaches. As former Pixar president Ed Catmull pointed out, "If you want to be original, you have to accept the uncertainty, even when it's uncomfortable."[4] Sticking to what we know can prove fatal when circumstances suddenly change. When a driver hits a patch of ice and the car starts to slide, the driver's first reaction is often to do what they do in other dangerous situations, hit the brakes. But hitting the breaks can actually make things worse. Instead, drivers need to work against their instincts and turn into the slide until they regain traction. Similarly, in disruptive situations, leaders often need to let go of what they think they know and try something new.

The siren song of certainty, though, is hard to ignore. This is particularly true when it comes to well-paid leaders whom others expect to have all the answers. Research shows that the longer a leader is in a job, the more certain and less curious they become.[5] David Chang, described in Chapter 3, remembers when he first started admitting to employees, "I don't know." His vulnerability ultimately empowered his team and fueled the organization's success. But employees' initial reaction was "It's doomsday. The leader doesn't know what to do."

Corporate life itself makes curiosity hard to pursue. The relentless focus on short-term goals and efficiency prompts leaders to move forward decisively without exploration. Admitting uncertainty invites critics and politics into decision-making and slows down initiatives. Meanwhile, investors and employees crave their own certainty, so leaders get pulled toward displaying greater confidence than they might actually feel.

Even though senior leaders say they value curiosity, they often impose certainty wherever they can, however superficially. They stay the course even when they suspect a problem, not just to avoid showing the vulnerability described in Chapter 3 but also to preserve their nicely ordered world and banish anxiety. The sunk-cost fallacy—stubbornly sticking with a failure because of all the money spent already—is only one example. Such head-in-the-sand persistence eventually takes the organization so far from reality that it results in disaster. In a volatile world, seeking certainty is a prescription for obsolescence.

The push for certainty is even more damaging in that it precludes true listening with colleagues. It trickles down and stifles discussion—two-thirds of employees say they face barriers to asking more questions at work.[6] Some leaders, even if they superficially stay positive and seek other's opinions, communicate opposition with their body language. Colleagues imagine them making mental notes that end up in a performance review down the line. Relationships suffer.

The quest for certainty doesn't just close off important information. It also leads organizations to concentrate their resources on the expected agenda. They look efficient and determined, but they're actually brittle because they're inward-facing and oblivious of the flow of outside events. Similar to the proverbial drunkard who looks for his keys only under the streetlight, certainty makes leaders and their organizations feel better but curtails their effectiveness. As Ray Hill, the CEO of CorEvitas points out, "Yes, you can project confidence and say, 'this is the way to go.' Your incentives are for leading with conviction. But chances are you're going to be wrong."[7]

The desire for certainty plays a role in most of the traps we discuss in the book. Leaders' convictions that they're right makes them less interested in relationships with others and less inclined to admit mistakes. It makes them more likely to impose their strategy top-down, emphasize efficiency over resilience, steamroll resistance to change, and adopt a hero mentality. And as we'll see in subsequent chapters, a desire for certainty also drives leaders to put their faith in best practices and data that may, in fact, lead them astray.

The Antidote to Certainty: Curiosity

What's the alternative? Curiosity, which leads to a continual pursuit of new information and perspectives. This drive to explore and learn inspires leaders to expand their knowledge and challenge their existing beliefs, resulting in a deeper understanding of how the world actually works.

Curiosity is as much a part of human nature as our desire for certainty. Conventional wisdom suggests that we are curious when we lack desired knowledge, because we are intrinsically motivated to explore and learn, or because we purposely seek out new, even extreme, experiences. In the 1950s, psychologist Daniel Berlyne provided the first overarching explanation. He maintained that everyone seeks a balance between two unpleasant states: boredom and over-stimulation. When we're bored, we look for things that interest us—we demonstrate curiosity. Alternatively, when we're overstimulated, we seek to reduce our state of arousal by finding answers that can help us make sense of what's going on.

In managing competing priorities and navigating market shifts, leaders, of course, are often overstimulated. Consequently, they must take care not to address the discomfort by looking only for information that confirms their existing views. Confirmation bias is an easy way of alleviating the leaders' unease, but it kills curiosity.

Studies suggest that as we age, we become less curious.[8] Additionally, in times of stress, we tend to double down on what we feel certain about rather than explore new options. Consequently, in an organizational crisis, senior leaders are more likely to impose their own certain views, instead of expressing curiosity, say, by asking questions or listening to others.

Yet leaders who let go of certainty and lean into curiosity benefit tremendously. Curiosity improves our analytical abilities. In the words of Harvard Business School professor Francesca Gino, "When our curiosity is triggered, we think more deeply and rationally about decisions."[9] Curiosity protects us from confirmation biases and keeps us opens to new possibilities.

Ray Hill remembers his effort to acquire a company that seemed a good fit for his and would lead to substantial growth: "I loved that company to death," he says. "I really wanted to make it happen and a lot of people would have just jumped at it." Hill knew, however, that many acquisitions fail, so he had his team do additional due diligence. "We went a lot deeper and a month later my thinking completely changed. I realized if we acquired them, it might actually have destroyed value for us." To his chagrin, he passed on what he initially felt confident was a plum target. It taught him that staying curious made for better decisions.[10]

Curiosity continues to matter even after we make decisions. Before a big decision, we often struggle over which option to choose. But afterwards, to reduce the discomfort we feel from choosing between different but viable options, our minds rationalize the decision we made. We come to believe it was "the obvious choice." The danger is that we then ignore new data that requires admitting we were wrong.

Staying curious keeps us open to new insights that can help us pivot if needed. One way leaders can keep an open mind is to ask themselves in advance of a decision, "How will I know if I made the wrong choice?" Alternatively, they can establish formal trip wires, such as a metric that they monitor, or they can schedule check-in-points, during which they review progress, to make sure they're still on the right course.

Additionally, curiosity fosters creativity, encouraging individuals to think in novel or unorthodox ways. From putting a man on the moon to sequencing the human genome, curiosity fuels innovation. Albert Einstein asserted that his genius wasn't the result of intelligence, famously stating, "I have no special talents. I am only passionately curious."[11]

Curiosity reduces defensiveness and increases empathy as well. The CEO at a global financial services company had a high-performing investment manager whom he was close with. The employee had young twin sons, one of whom identified as a girl, and who with the parents' support changed gender identity. The transition came as a shock to many in the organization, and it initially unsettled the CEO. He didn't understand it. Curious, he decided to learn more about gender identity and transition. As he read about others' experiences, he expanded his understanding of what "normal" meant. He came to respect the family's decision to raise the child as a girl and publicly supported the investment manager. Their relationship deepened, and instead of feeling marginalized, the investment manager rose steadily in the ranks. He added enormous value to the organization, far beyond his contribution to the company's culture of inclusion.

Research demonstrates that curiosity also increases tolerance to anxiety and uncertainty.[12] Instead of assuming the worst case, curiosity helps us to imagine more positive, alternative scenarios. Curiosity has a physiological effect as well. It stimulates the same reward centers in the brain as when we achieve a goal or learn something new. This can result in a release of dopamine, the neurotransmitter responsible for feelings of pleasure and joy.[13]

Curiosity can even make us more persuasive. In one study, participants were more likely to believe an expert when the expert stated that they were uncertain and expressed the need for more information. They were surprised when experts admitted uncertainty, which caused them to tune in and think more intently about what the expert was saying.[14]

For all of these reasons, those who assess executives for a living maintain that curiosity is one of the best overall predictors of leadership.[15] This, of course, doesn't mean that every situation necessitates the intellectual or organizational effort of sustained curiosity. But it does mean that leaders should make curiosity a fundamental value and foster it among their people. Curiosity, not a vain attempt to impose control, is the best way to address uncertainty in a volatile environment.

Cultivate a Curious Mindset

One way leaders can foster curiosity is by changing their mindsets. They can start by grounding themselves in gratitude. When we're afraid of the unknown, we focus on what we don't have, what won't work, and what will never change. But when we start from a place of gratitude, we become open to new ideas and possibilities. We fear change less, because we remember all the good things the world has delivered to us up to now.

This approach is similar to the idea of *growth mindset* developed by Stanford professor Carol Dweck. When we believe we can get better over time, we see changes as opportunities to learn and improve. Each challenge becomes not a test of our fundamental competence but a productive opportunity to stretch ourselves. It makes us open to exploring what this new situation has to offer us.

Leaders can work to reframe work, both their own and that of employees, to reflect a growth mindset. In cases such as customer safety, for example, near perfection should be the goal. But when creativity and innovation are critical, everyone should see challenges as an avenue for growth and feel safe to fail. In these cases, Harvard Business School professor Amy Edmondson advises framing the work as a learning challenge (developing capabilities, generating new ideas, proving or disproving hypotheses) versus an execution challenge (achieving targets, demonstrating competence, completing tasks). When leaders share that they value learning as much if not more than results, they free themselves and their employees up to be curious and try new things.

Often emotions get in the way of our curiosity. In some situations, the stakes just seem too high. Our anxiety and fear of failing, or looking foolish, make us cling to what we think we know. Leaders can reduce this challenge by distancing themselves from emotions and exploring new approaches.

Acknowledging and labeling emotions enables us to process them in a deliberate and conscious way so they don't consume us. Leaders can also ask themselves, "What would I tell my best friend to do?" or "What would my wiser, future-self tell me to do?" In doing so, they adopt an alternative, outside perspective that separates them from their emotions and forces them to think creatively and curiously.

A mindset of curiosity has an enormous secondary benefit these days. Especially in recent years with the "Great Resignation" and "quiet quitting," leaders are finding they can't take their internal organizations for granted any more than the external environment. Employee engagement has become a key challenge. A leader's curiosity inspires engagement, especially in dealing with mistakes. Leaders who know they are "right" are likely to pile on a colleague who fails at a task, relieved to have someone else to blame for any problems. They may move on and might even forget the event, but their chastened colleagues learn to act cautiously and stop exploring.

A curious leader doesn't take any failure at face value, but rather regards it as an opportunity to ask questions and learn. Some mistakes are simple matters of poor judgment that can, with reflection and effort, be remedied in the future. An old IBM joke puts it well. A manager blew an important project and lost $1 million in the process. He expected to be fired, but his boss said he had to stay; after all, "we just spent $1 million on your education."

Other failures arise when reality changes suddenly and unexpectedly. In these cases, leaders can dig below the what to the how and why, improving their ongoing assessment of markets. Many errors are thus productive failures, testing key hypotheses and yielding valuable information. And even unproductive mistakes can point to a larger problem in management training or organizational culture. When leaders value curiosity and a learning mindset, they and their colleagues no longer see one another as adversaries. Instead, they become engaged partners who help foster a better understanding of where markets are going.

The Importance of Understanding

What else can you do to foster curiosity and a learning mindset? One tactic is simply: seek out new information. Curious leaders are always digging into data and exploring different ways of thinking. They take the time to network with others who have different expertise and points of view. Similar to Ivan Berg in Chapter 2 on relationships, curious leaders aren't just interested in how their own portion of the business operates; they want to understand how it affects the broader enterprise. They read up on industry trends and look for weak signals in the external environment that may suggest which way the market is headed.

In their quest for new information, curious leaders probe the underlying drivers behind a situation, recognizing that a deeper analysis will lead to better insights and more effective solutions. Through this process, leaders can identify potential biases and blind spots and avoid decisions based on assumptions.

Toyota probes root causes with its Five Whys approach. Leaders ask why not just once, but five times. Most problems have multiple layers of causation, so the repeated questions get everyone drilling down to the fundamental factors at play.

Curious leaders apply their curiosity inwardly as well. We've seen several leaders continually seek feedback from colleagues about themselves. They deepen their understanding of how others perceive them and of areas where they can improve. For these leaders curiosity trumps ego. They set aside defensiveness in the pursuit of self-awareness and personal growth.

Communicating Curiosity

Leaders can also promote curiosity through their interactions with others and choice of language. As we describe in Chapter 3 on vulnerability, leaders model curiosity by acknowledging to others that they don't have the answer. Saying "I don't know" demonstrates humility and an openness to learning that invites others to share their ideas. Unfortunately, colleagues in many organizations can't take such humility and openness for granted. Many opportunities to cultivate curiosity as a value go untapped.

Leaders can also let others speak first. Too often leaders begin a conversation by saying, "Here's the problem, here's what I think we should do, what do you think?" This approach predetermines the flow of the discussion. Those with differing opinions find themselves in the unpleasant position of either keeping quiet or having to publicly disagree with the leader. If they do speak up, they likely couch their response: "That's a good idea but what if we tweak these few things." Fundamentally different ideas go unexpressed, diminishing creativity and alienating team members.

The real skill for leaders, according to organizational consultant Simon Sinek, is to keep a lid on their opinions. This is much harder than it sounds. Leaders are taught to speak up and advocate for their points of view. Keeping quiet takes courage. Without their input, conversations may go off in a direction that they disagree with. Alternatively, people may presume you have nothing valuable to add. But when leaders do hold back, everyone else feels heard, and the leader benefits from multiple perspectives.

Alfred Sloan, the CEO who built General Motors in the 1920s and 1930s, said he made a point of saying as little as possible in executive meetings. Only after hearing everyone's opinion did he speak up and make a decision.[16]

Even better, when leaders do choose to speak, it's often wise to start by asking questions rather than stating opinions. One scholar found that successful leaders ask as many as 10 questions for every declarative statement they make.[17] Asking questions helps in several ways. It demonstrates the leader's openness to others' opinions, which makes people feel valued. It communicates to colleagues that the leader views them not as tools but as fellow investigators. Colleagues become partners in curiosity rather than passive followers or opponents.

Second, asking questions elicits information and ideas that otherwise might never have surfaced, along with feedback that a leader might not expect. Ray Hill recalls a board meeting to review the company's strategy. The board was discussing which initiatives the organization might pursue when one director said, "Wait a second. Do you guys have the capacity to tackle all of this?" The question took the discussion in an entirely different direction, and the board worked with management to dramatically curtail the list of initiatives.

Third, asking questions causes people to think deeply. It encourages them to reflect, evaluate assumptions, identify connections and patterns, and consider different perspectives. That's why executive coaches often use questions, such as "What would you do if you were being your most courageous self?" or "How might you be contributing to this problem?" These questions help leaders to develop self-awareness, see beyond their existing paradigms, and expand the breadth of possible solutions.

Fourth, questions help leaders uncover information about why people believe what they believe and where they're coming from. When leaders understand why someone holds a certain opinion, they can see the issue from their perspective and appreciate their viewpoint. They can find common ground through empathy, which reduces conflict and boosts relationships. Some research suggests that the more questions you ask, the more colleagues will like you.[18]

Although the quantity of questions asked matters, so does the type. Follow-up questions demonstrate that you are paying attention and are interested in what the other person is saying. Open-ended questions (often starting with *what, how, when, where,* or *why*) are particularly good for generating new ideas, exploring complex issues, and encouraging critical thinking. For example, asking "How do you define public safety?" is likely to generate greater insight than simply asking "Should we defund the police?"

Closed-ended questions (those that can be answered with a simple yes or no) quickly establish facts or gather specific information, but they can also introduce bias. One study asked parents to name the most crucial skill to prepare children for life, choosing from a list of options. Sixty percent selected "thinking for themselves." But when the same question was posed in an open-ended format, only 5% mentioned this skill.[19]

The tone of questions also matters. To get authentic responses, leaders must not telegraph the "right" answer. Asking in a relaxed manner draws more candid responses, while a formal tone may hinder people's openness to sharing information.

Leaders can model curiosity even when they are sharing opinions or making recommendations. Before Doug Leeby became CEO of Beeline, an HR technology provider, he managed a division with multiple departments. Over time, he became frustrated that people were criticizing other departments while defending their own. The interactions were undermining trust and hurting collaboration, so Leeby decided to make a change.

He started the next executive team meeting by telling everyone, including himself, to begin statements with "I perceive." Instead of "You are being uncooperative," for example, someone might say, "I perceive we are having trouble working together." The tactic worked. Using *I* language framed the comments as a personal perspective, rather than a statement of universal fact. The resulting dialogue became more positive and constructive. Defensiveness decreased and relationships across the team improved even after Leeby stopped insisting on the practice.

With all of these tactics, the key step is to acknowledge that you as the leader simply don't have all the answers. When you start off by admitting you don't know and ask questions, you'll probably know a lot more by the end of the meeting than if you began with confident assertions.

Keep Reassessing

Yet another way leaders can increase their curiosity is by continually refining their assumptions. Responding to the failure of intelligence agencies to predict the 9/11 attacks, the US Congress in 2006 created the Intelligence Advanced Research Projects Agency (IARPA) and charged it with conducting bold, innovative research. Wondering if it could use the wisdom of the crowd to help predict future events, IARPA launched a huge public forecasting tournament in 2011. Thousands of people started making predictions on a series of questions, such as "Will North Korea launch a new multi-stage missile before May 10, 2014?" Groups that didn't hit certain benchmarks for accuracy were eliminated over time. By the tournament's fourth year, one team was clearly outperforming the rest and, in some cases, even beating IARPA's internal team, which had access to classified information.

The team, named Good Judgment, was led by Philip Tetlock and Barbara Mellers from the University of Pennsylvania. In studying what set the team apart, researchers learned that the single best indicator of someone's ability to forecast isn't smarts or access to information. It is the frequency with which they are willing to tweak their forecasts as new information comes in—and even to seek out that information. One Good Judgment team member, for example, went so far as to hunt down a spokesperson for the Muslim Brotherhood to get the inside track on a question about Egypt.[20] Tetlock and his coauthor call this *perpetual beta*—the extent to which someone goes to continually update and improve their assessment. Tetlock maintains this trait is "roughly three times as powerful a predictor as its closest rival, personal intelligence."[21]

The use of the OKR (objectives and key results) goal setting and management framework is one way leaders can apply a perpetual beta inside their companies. As described in Chapter 4 on combining strategy and execution, OKRs encourage leaders and their teams to continually reassess what's working and what's not and update their approach accordingly. It forces leaders to stay curious.

Escaping the Trap

Much of the work of leaders in the past was about building regularity in otherwise messy markets. But that highly gratifying work is now a fool's errand. Instead of doubling down on certainty in a misguided effort to regain control, leaders today must draw on curiosity as a coping mechanism for ongoing change. Similar to George at the opening of this chapter, it's better to accept the uncertainty, lean into curiosity, and increase your ability to see what's really going on. When leaders let go of the need for certainty and shift into a curious mindset, they stop trying to predict the future—an increasingly futile task—and instead create a state of organizational readiness. That in turn enables them to adapt more effectively over time.

10 Data-Driven Decisions Still Need a Driver

Team-building meetings are often forgettable, but not the one that one of us (Dan) facilitated many years ago. Prior to the meeting, the executives completed an online survey assessing their team's strengths and development opportunities. Dan and his colleagues crunched the data and produced the results, which were surprisingly negative. It appeared the team rated itself quite low on indices related to how much they trusted one another and were open to engaging in candid conversations.

The CEO was taken aback by the results and said he had no idea people felt this way. Team members began to share their theories on why the scores were low, raising specific examples of when they witnessed maladaptive behavior. Many reported that the ensuing discussion was the most candid and productive conversation the team ever had. To a person, the executives felt they had grown closer as a team.

After a festive team dinner, Dan returned to his hotel for the evening, pleased with how the day had gone. But something was gnawing at him. He went back to the survey data and was mortified to discover that in the rush to process the survey data he and his colleagues had inverted the scales. Where he had told the leadership team their ratings were high, they were low, and vice versa. Dan called the CEO to confess the error and explain the situation. Expecting the CEO would chew him out, Dan was pleasantly surprised.

"Dan," the CEO replied, "that was the best discussion about our team we ever had. The data was irrelevant. It was the conversation that mattered."

Contrast the story with that of another company, led by a smart, aggressive executive team. Leaders on this team prided themselves on taking their cue from the data, whether the information came from macroeconomic indicators, operational databases, or employee surveys. The trouble was that they treated data differently depending on whether the information fit their expectations.

If the data supported what they had in mind, they proceeded aggressively, making decisions and developing plans. When the data told a different story, particularly in sensitive subjects such as resource allocation or talent assessments, the discussion shifted. How big was the sample size? Let's see the wording on that survey instrument. Did the data cover a full period or just a few days? What are the benchmarks? And what about the margin of error?

When they didn't like the data, they quibbled with every aspect, poking holes in the methodology, until they decided the information wasn't reliable. At that point they threw it out and went with their initial gut, even if the data were still useful directionally. Or they got stuck in analysis paralysis, with endless arguments about the data's validity and what additional information they needed to decide. Often these leaders deferred any decision until the next meeting, when they would have "better" data.

When Data Deceives

As we've seen, leaders are desperate for certainty in complex environments and data seem to offer the requisite clarity. It appears wonderfully precise, scientific, neutral, impersonal, free of politics. Leaders are stuck making tough decisions on where to go in the fog of markets, balancing claims from throughout an organization.

For leaders sinking in a mess of competing priorities, data offer a seemingly secure rope.

Moreover, we've gotten much better at creating and collecting data. The digital transformation of most companies has yielded a flood of information for leaders to analyze. That data may need to be cleaned, sorted, and analyzed, but consultants promise that's a doable task.

Data also ensure accountability to the present, which is one reason private equity firms tend to oversee their portfolio companies by insisting on mustering data whenever making a major decision. In projecting sales or expenses, for example, it's easy for leaders to estimate from their gut, but that intuition is susceptible to confirmatory and other biases. Data help to validate our assumptions and connect our estimates to what's actually happening in the real world.

About 2000, a division at a large IT company started creating a virtual shopping mall. The investment was a complete disaster, partly because the company didn't have market permission to act as a mall operator. But mostly it failed because it tried to map an old construct—malls—onto the new post-mall world. Most brands, it turned out, wanted to build their own online identities. The division proceeded with the plan until they found they couldn't get enough retailer commitments for critical mass. If its leaders had insisted on data before making a major investment, they would have greatly limited their losses.

Taking that point a step further, leaders also like data because the information lets them off the hook for tough decisions. They can say they simply did what the data suggested. Who can fault them?

Much of the history of management has been a steady move toward greater rationality and the use of evidence, away from personal power, ego, and intuition. Since the rise of systematic management in the early 20th century, through management accounting mid-century and then data analytics at the turn of the century, successive generations of leaders have drawn on new methods and tools. And now with big data and machine learning, organizations have ever more ways to "modernize" based on hard evidence. With our unimaginably powerful methods of collecting, storing, and analyzing data, leaders have much more to work with than ever before. No wonder the first instinct of most leaders is to ask, "What does the data show?"

Yet data's sheer attractiveness also entraps leaders. With data in hand, leaders think they have control over a situation. They want to lower risk so much that they overlook data's limitations, which are many.

The first is that data are based on history. Although we can use data to predict the future, these predictions assume the future looks like the past. In turbulent environments, that's often not the case. Consequently, data can lead us astray.

One leader barely avoided this trap while heading the banking services division of a large IT company. It was 2000 and his division was booming, closing 1,000 contracts a week. Extensive metrics showed that the sales pipeline was strong. But that year many industries, especially banking, began moving to the new world of online services. This leader's customers just hadn't gotten around to adjusting their purchasing, so all that wonderful pipeline data reflected the past, not the future. Fortunately, he gleaned the true trend from salespeople, "I know what customers are sending in purchase orders for," they told him, "but I also know what conversations they're having, and it's not that; it's about online banking."

A leader focused on data could have ignored those statements as mere anecdotes. Fortunately, this one took the statements to heart and changed course in time to capitalize on the emerging market.

In a complex world, big decisions should depend on much more than hard data. Leaders should consider discussions with clients and colleagues, external thought leaders, and intuition. Gerd Gigerenzer, managing director of the Max Planck Institute for Human Development, observes that relying on data analytics is "a good strategy if you have a business in a very stable world. . . . But if you deal with an uncertain world, big data will provide an illusion of certainty. . . . You need something else."[1]

Just look at all the tech companies, from Netflix to Microsoft and Meta, that expanded their payrolls enormously during the pandemic, when demand was heavy. Their reliance on backward-looking data lead them to mistakenly assume "permanent acceleration," which by early 2023 resulted in large-scale layoffs.[2] As Ryan Petersen, co-CEO of Flexport, points out, "If the future doesn't look like the past, being data-driven actually is not really helping you that much."[3]

Data are also imperfect, because flawed people collect and manage the information. Even sophisticated Amazon, which relies on data to achieve hyper-efficient distribution, has admitted to serious mistakes. A lack of information sharing between HR systems resulted in what one journalist called a "hellscape," in which automated systems shut off employees' disability benefits without notice and automatically fired those on approved leave.[4]

Likewise, imperfect people write the algorithms that assess the data, and any biases in those algorithms distort the results. Portions of the US criminal justice system rely on risk models that predict the likelihood that someone will commit another crime. Judges use those models in setting bail, sentencing, and probation. But the models rely heavily on rates of rearrests, which we've learned can have more to do with policing practice than individuals' inherent criminality.[5] As a result, judges risk setting sentences based on "objective" data that are actually biased.

Leaders are especially drawn to quantitative data, which they see as reliable, free from personal bias or subjective interpretation. Numbers seem precise and accurate, but they can still come from biased sources or flawed or manipulated logic.

Meta had to stop its demo of Galactica, a machine learning system trained on 48 million scientific sources, after two days because of outrage over the system generating misinformation.[6] The statements in question seemed "scientific," but experts knew the difference and called out the problem.

Even reliable data typically require specialized expertise. But many companies lack a systematic, accessible structure for managing the data they collect. "They're like libraries with no card catalog and no covers on their books," says Shvetank Shah, former leader of the Corporate Executive Board's information technology practice, and his colleagues.[7]

Reliance on data also slows decisions, as leaders wait for still more data to be collected and analyzed. Neurologists tell us that information is addicting—all the more so, we might add, for anxious leaders looking for an anchor. They always want more, but more is never enough. Richard Abdoo, chair and CEO of Wisconsin Energy Corporation, summarizes the result: "at the point when you've gathered enough data to be 99.99% certain that the decision you're about to make is the correct one, that decision has become obsolete."[8] The relentless pursuit of data traps leaders into inaction and withers their powers of judgment.

One indication that leaders are falling into this trap is their insistence on benchmarks. They can't interpret data, they claim, unless they know the "average" or "standard" level for a metric in their industry or peer group. As with the trap of best practice (described in Chapter 11), leaders find safety in knowing the benchmarks and working in that direction, even if doing so constricts the company's strategy or relegates the organization to the mean. Yet what works for many companies may not work for their organization.

Finally, data usually requires judgment to generate insight. Data can say a great many things—but rarely does it force a specific understanding or conclusion. Instead of substituting for judgment, it puts a premium on judgment to make sense of the information. Our friend and Duke professor Tony O'Driscoll points out, you need to contextualize data—to put it "in formation"—before it becomes meaningful (footnote). This process of model-building, or sense-making, which we discuss further in chapter 11, is as important to generating insight as the underlying data itself.

Yet, the knowledge and skills needed to analyze the data and derive meaning from it are difficult to integrate. Leaders often lack the analytical capabilities to discern data quality and properly explore the data. Thus, companies are stuck relying on outside data experts. This resulting gap in understanding—between managers who understand the business but not the data, and data scientists who understand the data but not the business—makes it challenging to draw conclusive findings. This gap is exacerbated when experts build black box models that prevent testing against experience and practical knowledge.[9]

As a result, data-driven decisions can have dangerous consequences, such as encouraging people to focus on the wrong problems. When Wells Fargo leaders began highlighting the bank's low rates of cross-selling, they started a process that shifted how managers worked with customer-facing staff members. As with students learning narrowly because of instructors teaching to the test, employees focused on hitting their cross-selling goals, not on what customers actually needed or on what was good for the bank in the long run. The result was a scandal that cost the bank billions of dollars in fines and lost goodwill.

Seeing Beyond the Numbers

Data are fundamental to managing in the modern economy. The challenge is doing so without becoming trapped by data. One solution is to broaden the kind of data sought. Leaders tend to prefer quantitative, easily compared numbers that clearly show changes over time. But an increasing number of decisions depend on areas often served with qualitative as well as quantitative data, such as brand image, customer tendencies or, as discussed, employee engagement. Leaders need to understand how people are thinking, not just actions reducible to simple numbers. Qualitative data provide rich and in-depth information about people's experiences, perceptions, and attitudes. It helps to uncover underlying rationales, motivations, and emotions that are not easily measurable through quantitative data.

As president of education solutions at Scholastic, Rose Else-Mitchell has worked with both kinds of data. "You can't let good be the enemy of perfect," she points out, by insisting on hard data.

The numbers can look good even when interviews with users point to dissatisfaction that will hurt future sales. To reduce this risk, she and her colleagues have set up an innovation laboratory that commissions ethnographic research on how children interact with reading materials.

Quantitative blinders are a problem for data sent out to customers as well. One of Scholastic's major products is a magazine reprinting articles of interest to schoolchildren, now in digital as well as print form. The digital version had the advantage of recording how long kids engaged with each issue, and the company was quick to make use of it. "In our eagerness to give teachers and districts information on how much they were using the materials," Else-Mitchell points out, "we made a big deal about time of use, which as it turns out doesn't give you the full scope of how kids actually use the product." Quantitative data can narrow the attention of leaders and everyone else to what can easily be measured, at the cost of understanding the full reality.[10]

Even qualitative data can be a trap for anxious leaders. But because "soft" data require more judgment to interpret, that type of information can reduce the likelihood of a leader putting data in the driver's seat.

Along with broadening the data, leaders need to make sure the data represent the reality of the marketplace. The talent acquisition function at one company was excited to share that the average time to fill an open position was only 65 days: half the industry benchmark. Business leaders in the organizations were incredulous. The inability to hire was curtailing their operations and hurting customer satisfaction. Were they really two times better at hiring than their competitors? How could that be?

As it turned out, they weren't. More analysis uncovered that talent acquisition had a policy of closing and reopening unfilled requisitions after 100 days, restarting the clock each time. Additionally, if a business leader needed to hire five people to do the same job, talent acquisition opened only one requisition at a time, waiting to open the next until the previous one was filled.

The talent acquisition department wasn't trying to manipulate the numbers. They were doing the best job they could. They'd learned that positions that were open too long fell to the bottom of the list on online recruiting sites. Closing and reopening a job requisition bumped it back up to the top of the list where it was more likely to be seen by candidates. Also, prospective hires got nervous when they saw many open positions. It made them worry that the company couldn't hold on to employees. Thus, it was better to only recruit for one position versus all five at a time.

The moral of the story: data can provide a misleading picture. The picture can change dramatically depending on your point of view.

The Hidden Strength of Intuitive Leaders

Leaders can further avoid the data trap by applying their intuition. Too often leaders think they should downplay their gut, but data should inform their judgment, not the other way around. As Einstein said, "The intuitive mind is a sacred gift and the rational mind is a faithful servant. We have created a society that honors the servant and has forgotten the gift."[11]

Intuition as we're considering it here is not a wild irrational sense, but rather a predictable kind of pattern matching. Scientists believe our unconscious minds make judgments by sifting through long-term memory to identify previous experiences that reflect the current moment. The result is a powerful tool. Researchers have found that different professions such as firefighters, soldiers, and neonatal intensive care nurses routinely use intuition to make life-saving decisions in the absence of data.

Similar examples abound in business. When COVID hit, many companies began cutting costs and hoarding cash. But the software and computer peripheral company Logitech chose to invest in inventory. It was a wise decision. As CEO Bracken Darrell noted in 2021, "We grew 74% last year because we had inventory to sell. . . . I won't pretend we were geniuses. We just followed our intuition. Now it seems obvious."[12]

Intuition is particularly critical to innovation, where complexity abounds and leaders frequently encounter new situations. In 1988, Chrysler was struggling with products that critics called technologically dated and uninspired. One weekend, Bob Lutz, then the company's president, took his Cobra roadster for a spin. As he raced along the roads in southeastern Michigan, he felt guilty that he was driving a car with an engine made by Ford, a competitor and his former employer.

Lutz knew that Chrysler didn't have a V-8 engine up to snuff for a roadster, but it did have a powerful 10-cylinder engine in development for a pickup truck, with an optional five-speed manual transmission. Despite skepticism from others, he decided to co-opt those monster parts for a sexy, expensive, two-seat concept sports car. The Dodge Viper became a smashing success. It single-handedly changed the public's perception of Chrysler, dramatically boosting company morale, providing desperately needed momentum, and fueling Chrysler's dramatic turnaround in the 1990s.

Lutz had trouble describing how he made one of the most critical decisions of his career. "It was this subconscious visceral feeling. And it just felt right." He justified the gutsy move by using an analogy. "When you're going too slow in an airplane, your aerodynamic drag builds up because the nose of the airplane is positioned too high and you can actually get to the point where, even at full power, you can't get the airplane to climb anymore. So your only solution is to drop the nose and trade off some altitude to gain speed." Similarly, Chrysler in the late 1980s had lost so much momentum that it was in danger of stalling. The conventional wisdom called for cost cutting to gain altitude, not spending cash on a frivolous vehicle like the Dodge Viper. But Lutz's intuition knew better.[13]

Intuition has the enormous advantage of working much faster than careful data analysis. Speed is particularly important in complex environments. Ralph Larsen, former CEO of Johnson & Johnson, said it best: "Often there is absolutely no way that you could have the time to thoroughly analyze every one of the options or alternatives available to you. So you have to rely on your business judgment."

That's especially true for leaders, as Larsen goes on to explain: "Very often, people will do a brilliant job up through the middle management levels, where it's very heavily quantitative in terms of the decision-making. But then they reach senior management, where the problems get more complex and ambiguous."[14]

Combining Hard Data and Gut Feeling

As we've suggested, smart leaders rely on neither data or intuition alone. Rather, they integrate them. Data provide a potentially objective view of a situation, but with limited context or nuanced understanding of complex issues. Intuition, however, draws on past experiences, emotions, and gut feelings to provide a subjective view.

Yet the predictive models of big data methodologies rarely incorporate a manager's unique knowledge of the business. Paolo Gaudiano, cofounder and chief scientist at Aleria, argues, "This is tantamount to someone collecting a lot of data and then deciding to throw away half of it—except in this case you are arguably throwing away the more valuable half, because the manager has specific knowledge of the business, while the data science approaches are generic."[15]

Leaders who integrate data with intuition perform better. In one study, The Corporate Executive Board evaluated 5,000 employees at 22 global companies and sorted them into three different groups. "Unquestioning empiricists" trusted analysis over judgment, while "visceral decision-makers" went exclusively with their gut. It was the third group, "informed skeptics" who balanced judgment and analysis, who made the best decisions. What's more, functions with the most informed skeptics had close to 25% better productivity, employee engagement, and market share growth. Yet only half of senior managers fell into the informed skeptic category.[16]

Let Context Be Your Guide

Part of balancing the use of data and intuition is knowing when to use them. Amazon teaches employees to differentiate between one-way-door and two-way-door decisions. Two-way-door decisions are those you can easily reverse; you can walk back through them. These are decisions to make quickly, based on judgment or intuition. One-way-door decisions are much harder to reverse. Because the risk is higher, these decisions warrant extensive data and analysis.

As organizations grow, they tend to treat more and more decisions as one-way-door decisions. This slows down the organization and diminishes creativity and innovation. Jeff Bezos told his shareholders in 2020, "Most decisions should probably be made with somewhere around 70 percent of the information you wish you had. If you wait for 90 percent, in most cases, you're probably being slow." For Bezos, speed and the ability to recognize you made a mistake and course correct are more important than having perfect information at the start. He goes on to say, "Being wrong may be less costly than you think, whereas being slow is going to be expensive for sure.[17]

Similarly, knowledge management expert Dave Snowden and his colleague distinguish among multiple decision-making contexts, three of which are simple, complicated, complex.[18] Simple contexts are stable, with clear cause and effect. Consequently, the right answer is typically self-evident. Here leaders can confidently apply "best practices" (the topic of Chapter 11). Complicated contexts still have clear relationships between cause and effect, but these are harder to see. Often, leaders need to collect and analyze relevant data or bring in experts in order to make sense of what's going on and define an appropriate path forward.

In complex contexts, however, cause and effect are ever-changing. Snowden contrasts a Ferrari and a rainforest to illustrate the differences between complicated and complex circumstances. A Ferrari is complex. It's like a puzzle with many moving parts. You need an expert to diagnose and fix a problem. But a Ferrari is also static.

The relationships between the parts don't change. As a result, the process to fix it on a Tuesday morning is the same as the process to fix it on Saturday afternoon, and it doesn't change if you move the car from Milan to London. By contrast, a rainforest is dynamic, in a constant state of flux. The relationships among the animals, ecology, geology, and weather continually evolve. Adding or removing a species can have radically different effects on the broader rainforest depending on the conditions (e.g., weather, migration patterns, time of year) at the specific moment in time.

Similar to the rainforest, most businesses today operate in a complex context. Regulatory changes, new leadership, acquisitions, and layoffs all have unpredictable and unintended consequences. In this environment, we can't know what the impact of our actions will be until after we perform them. The bad news, then, is that data, because the information is derived from the past, becomes less helpful.

Understanding context is critical for leaders when choosing how to leverage data. If you are making a high-risk decision in a relatively stable environment and have access to data and time to analyze, then by all means do so. But if you're operating in a complex environment, or can revisit the decision down the road, then it's often better to forgo analysis and rely on expertise and judgment. As David Chang, president and chief technology officer of WuXi AppTec's Advanced Therapies Unit, remarks, "Sometimes there is no good data, and you just need to act based on judgment. Any decision is often better than no decision. Three months later you can revisit most decisions and you'll have the benefit of hindsight."[19]

Indeed, the answer to turbulence and ambiguity isn't to put data in the driver seat but to complement it with intuition based on experience. Here we can learn from Magnus Carlsen, world chess champion since 2013 and the highest-rated player of all time. Most players come to world championships after countless hours of study with chess-playing software. They learn the optimal moves in the most probable situations. Carlsen takes a different approach. Among grandmasters, Carlsen uses computers the least to improve his play, preferring to build up his own evaluative skills, his human touch—and to use other players' reliance on data-driven computers against them. He is so inventive that his best move is often a suboptimal one. He leads his opponents down obscure paths that no existing data set would prepare them for. As a result, they get lost and make mistakes.[20]

A Shortcut with Heuristics

One way leaders can sidestep analysis paralysis is by defining heuristics, rules of thumb or reliable shortcuts for making decisions. These come from a combination of experience, observation, and generalization.

Heuristics are particularly useful when leaders face a flood of information and have a short window in which to decide. They can map a relevant, existing heuristic onto the situation to determine an appropriate course of action. An example is firefighters' application of "risk a lot to save a lot, risk a little to save a little, risk nothing to save nothing." On their arrival at a fire, incident commanders use such heuristics to make decisions that balance the risk to firefighters against the potential for saving civilians.[21]

Heuristics are common in the business world. These include Amazon's two-way-door and one-way-door decisions, and Toyota's Five Whys described in Chapter 9. Microsoft recently introduced a heuristic to manage the accumulation of bugs during software development. Previously, engineers would wait until the end of the development cycle to fix bugs, but this approach often resulted in a never-ending cycle of fixing bugs only to find more—a process that prolonged the launch schedule. So the company established a "bug cap" rule, calculated using the formula: number of engineers × 5. If the bug count exceeds the cap, the development team stops working on new features and focuses on reducing the bug count. The heuristic has enabled the company to release products more quickly as the bugs are minimized during each product's development.[22]

Much quicker than analyzing reams of data, heuristics often yield outcomes that are just as effective.[23] That's because heuristics are often based on the most relevant information for a particular decision or problem, rather than a comprehensive analysis of all available data. Moreover, although heuristics are not guaranteed to produce the perfect solution, in today's complex environment there is seldom, if ever, a single right answer. And, as Jeff Bezos argues, speed is often the most important factor.

Leaders need to be keenly aware of the potential for biases to creep into their heuristics. A company that relies solely on graduates from prestigious universities as its recruitment pool runs the risk of introducing systematic bias into its hiring process. This approach assumes that these candidates are the most intelligent, but it overlooks the fact that intelligence and potential are not solely determined by one's educational background. In addition, the narrow focus on a single criterion can lead to a homogeneous workforce that lacks diversity in skills, experiences, and perspectives, which can limit the company's ability to innovate and adapt to change.

Influencing Others

Leaders feel drawn to data because the information cuts through the noise to get to the heart of the matter. But that benefit comes with a cost, in that it removes emotion from the conversation.

Researchers have found that emotion is essential to decision-making. In one study, when people with a tumor in the area of the brain responsible for emotion were presented with a dilemma, they could come up with potential solutions but were unable to choose between them.[24] Our emotions signal to us what's important, provide motivation for action, and facilitate memory.

Integrating emotion into an argument is also a far more effective way of influencing others. People maintain their own set of authorities, statistics, and facts. Consequently, while you're trying to persuade them with data, they're debating you in their own heads.

When we employ emotion we involve the listener, generating empathy and causing them to perceive the situation from our perspective.

One of our colleagues went for a hike with a new friend. Based on what he knew of her interests, he assumed she shared his political views. During their discussion, he learned that she was a gun owner. As a strong proponent of gun control, he was surprised. When he asked her why, she shared that she had previously been the victim of a stalker and lived in the woods by herself far from the nearest police station. Given her experience and current circumstances she felt safer knowing she could protect herself. Our colleague recalls, "The story and the emotion it conveyed made me reconsider my point of view in a way data or statistics never would have."

Similarly, data tends to reduce the rich totality of a story to a few metrics. The discussion becomes a one-way sharing of information.

Alan Mulally, who directed engineering for Boeing's 777 project before becoming CEO of Ford, said, "When you're creating something, you have to recognize that it's the interaction that will allow everybody to come to a fundamental understanding."[25] Discussion creates comprehension and trust in ways that information sharing on its own does not.

Data often push people to focus on numbers rather than relationships or purpose, particularly when the data involve a power relationship. If people know their bosses will judge them on a certain metric, they'll feel tempted to misreport the data to improve their results. Worse, they may act in ways that ultimately work against the company's interests. A large bonus tied to the share price might induce a CEO to favor short-term spending over long-term investment. It's too easy for data to get in the way of seeing what's really going on in the company. People stop paying attention to what's important and focus on the data.

Data can still be a useful way to communicate ideas to others. But by itself data discourage connection. Leaders need to connect the numbers to the big picture and clarify that these are only a starting point for a conversation. Alternatively, if the goal is to persuade, they must situate the data within a compelling narrative—an emotional story that explains why the data matter and respects where the colleague is coming from.

Leaders will always need to gather and use data. Information grounds us in reality, provides feedback on what's working, and, as in the virtual mall idea, counters biases. Evidence-based management would be an improvement over the gut-based decisions of many organizations. But rather than falling prey to the illusion that data provide the perfect answer, or using the information to reduce their anxiety about uncertainty, leaders must apply data selectively. It's just one part of arriving at and communicating decisions in a way that builds organizational strength, not undermines it.

Escaping the Trap

The world is awash in data, and the Internet of Things, 5G networks, and AI models will only accelerate data's exponential growth rate. It's not surprising that leaders eager for certainty continue to believe they'll find the right answer if they just look hard enough.

But, although data can inform us, it can also ensnare us. It's often better to be fast and able to change course than to collect all the data needed to be sure you're right. Moreover, data by its very nature is often retrospective. Would the iPad exist if Apple CEO Steve Jobs had relied solely on the many market analysts who reported that tablets would never make a dent in the PC market?

Like Magnus Carlsen, leaders need not let data dominate their judgment. There's simply no substitute for the leader who combines all kinds of insight and information, including data, with intuition, experience, and creativity. To navigate the turbulent and ambiguous environment of the modern world, leaders must be willing to take risks, make mistakes, and learn from failure. They must be willing to challenge conventional wisdom and question assumptions, rather than simply relying on data to confirm what they already believe to be true. In many cases, the most innovative and successful leaders are those who are willing to take a leap of faith based on their own judgment and intuition, rather than simply following the data.

11

When Best Isn't Best

3M used to be synonymous with innovation. The company trans-formed itself from a commodity maker of sandpaper to one with popular products from Scotchgard fabric protection to Post-It notes and CFC-free asthma inhalers. Then in 2001 a new leader, former GE executive Jim McNerney, joined the company with goals of improving it further.

In three years, he converted the entire company to Six Sigma, a system of best practices for improving quality by reducing errors in operations. McNerney's plan worked at first, as quality improved and costs fell. But by mid-2005, when McNerney left to become CEO of Boeing, 3M's rate of innovation had fallen sharply. McNerney's application of best practices had undermined one of the company's most important competitive advantages.

The root of the problem was Six Sigma's insistence on plans and discipline, which discourages work on novel products. Geoff Nicholson, father of the Post-It note, had just retired as vice president for international technical operations as McNerney arrived. He pinpointed the problem: "The Six Sigma people would say they need a five-year business plan for [a new idea]. Come on, we don't know yet because we don't know how it works, we don't know how many customers, we haven't taken it out to the customer yet."[1] McNerney's successor, George Buckley, largely discontinued the use of Six Sigma in research and development.[2] 3M's leader had fallen into a trap, but you don't have to. Often, best practices really aren't best for individual companies. Sometimes they aren't even close.

The Hidden Cost of "Best" Practices

Business leaders the world over believe strongly that the quickest way to boost performance is to uncover the strategies of successful businesses and adopt them. Why not? Adopting best practices appears to be a shortcut to excellence; it frees companies from having to reinvent the wheel.

Best practices also provide legitimacy. They make people feel safe and secure. And in stable environments, leaders can identify causal relationships and connect their challenges with general frameworks. It makes sense to work from one of the popular strategic practices, such as Porter's Five Forces, McKinsey's 7 S, or BCG's growth matrix.

While those frameworks were becoming commonplace, consultants also played up specific "best practices" for every client to follow. Nervous executives gravitated toward these approaches because they entailed less risk. Who could criticize you if you were doing what's "best"? And why think for yourself if you can just apply a tried-and-true approach? If you're running a big company in a predictable environment, you'll naturally tend to play it safe and just put your abundant resources to work on executing.

Yet best practices have enormous downsides. First, they are one-size-fits-all approaches. The truth is that every organization has its own unique challenges and circumstances. As we saw in the case of 3M, just because a practice works in one environment doesn't mean leaders can apply it elsewhere. Moreover, even if successfully implemented, best practices undermine differentiation, which is essential to sustained success in a competitive economy. They promote a herd mentality, where those who follow along are just playing catch-up. Over time, best practices encourage a giant regression to the mean.

Best practices also change over time. In the 1990s, many companies embraced the stack or "forced ranking" popularized by General Electric. Managers evaluated their employees on a fixed curve, with set percentages labeled as top, average, and underperformers. The goal was to identify the weaker performers and either improve or fire them. Over time, leaders came to recognize that the practice created a toxic work environment—employees competed against each other and declined to collaborate—and they relegated it to the waste bin.

Likewise, in the 1990s many believed that stock-based compensation would align leaders' interests with those of investors. Experts argued that management would then run companies to maximize shareholder value. But this dominant orthodoxy resulted in disasters at Enron, Global Crossing, Tyco International, Qwest Communications, and several "dot-bombs." In each case, executives made speculative moves that temporarily boosted stock prices but added little real value. Not surprisingly, many experts now advise curtailing the practice.

Quite often, "best" practices often simply aren't. We tend to confuse correlation for causation. Just because Elon Musk and Jeff Bezos both eat dinner every night doesn't make it a best practice of successful leaders. And these judgments often flow from a tiny sample. We make a big deal about successes, but rarely track when a best practice doesn't work. Leaders at companies that succeeded with a particular practice appear at conferences talking about their experiences. But what about those who did exactly the same practice and failed? We don't hear about them.

As many consultants know, you can find a best practice that supports almost any position. You can find, for example, best practices that advocate for promoting employees based on their potential, as well as best practices that insist you promote only employees with a track record of strong performance. It just depends on where you look and whom you ask.

Most "best practices" have always been merely the judgment of consultants and others who see multiple organizations struggling over a common challenge. They take whatever practice seems most effective lately in dealing with that issue and deem it a "best practice" to convince clients to go along. The label addresses the insecurities of clients, but rarely have any consultancies gone to the trouble of rigorously determining the "best."

The easiest way to understand this problem is to look at the notorious tendency of much-praised companies to falter over time. *In Search of Excellence*, the 1982 mega-best-seller by Tom Peters and Robert Waterman, praised several firms for their "bias for action," "staying close to customers," "sticking to the knitting," along with five other behaviors. Ten years later, most of those praiseworthy firms, such as Atari, had fallen out of favor. Peters confessed that they had proceeded first by asking consultants which companies were doing "cool things." Then they came up with quantitative metrics to justify the selection, and only then called out behaviors that seemed to propel that success.

Similar problems beset the firms in *Built to Last: Successful Habits of Visionary Companies* (Collins & Porras, 1994) and *What Really Works* (Murawski & Scott, 2004). Despite the appearance of data and rigor, most of the insights came from qualitative evidence obscured by the "halo effect." When companies succeed, they gain press coverage trying to explain their success in substantive ways, even when the success may have come largely from luck. Over time, most lucky companies revert to the mean.

Best practices also come with hidden costs. Switching to a new approach can be extremely disruptive. One study of large US companies adopting best practices in IT found that performance initially dipped and only started to improve after the third year.[3] In another study, researchers examined five different management models for Silicon Valley startups and found that one—the commitment model—clearly outperformed the others. But startups that sought to switch to the commitment model after launch were three times more likely to fail.[4]

Perhaps most damaging, best practices often alienate employees. Bringing in outside ideas essentially tells the organization that what they're doing now is substandard, outdated, or ignorant. It turns them into the benighted colleagues needing a wise leader to rescue them with a better approach.

Early in his career, Tom Bigda-Peyton, the former head of learning for Catholic Health, presented some of his ideas as "best practice." He found that he was setting up competition right off the bat. His colleagues essentially said, "Well, we weren't waiting for you. And now you're bringing in a best practice. Got any interest in what we're already doing anyway?"

Psychological barriers arose that discouraged people from even trying out the proposed idea. Bigda-Peyton realized that calling something *best practice* prevented the learning and customization that every organization needs to succeed with an idea. After all, if it's truly a "best practice," why would you ever customize it? It's already the best!

From then on, Bigda-Peyton made a point of never referring to *best practices*. Instead, when he heard about an interesting idea from outside his organization, he called it a *promising practice*. He would tell colleagues, "Here's something we discovered; we think it might work for you. But we don't know that for sure. Why don't we try it out, evaluate, and learn from it?" According to Bigda-Peyton, "Talking about it as a promising practice encourages adaptation versus just jamming a square peg into a round hole."[5]

Complexity Confounds the Problem

As markets become more volatile, best practices become even less helpful. To apply them properly, you first need a thorough understanding of the problem. But in complex settings, it's almost impossible to scope out problems well enough to apply best practices with confidence. Instead of simply finding and implementing best practice, complexity demands a nimbler approach, one in which you pursue a direction, see if it works, and adapt in response until you get to your destination.

As the environment grows more complex, organizations also become more unique, customizing their strategy, structure, and processes to address their specific circumstances. This means that what works in one place likely won't work elsewhere unless managers at the latter do the hard work of translating the practice. As John Seely Brown and Paul Duguid point out in *The Social Life of Information*, knowledge tends to be "sticky" and not as easy to transfer as we might hope. That's why Toyota was comfortable allowing rivals to tour their factories. They knew that it would take many years for any company to copy its famed lean production system.

Don DeGolyer, the founder and former CEO of Vertice Pharma and former CEO of Sandoz, maintains, "It's important to understand those 'best practices,' but you still have to be flexible and adapt to the situation." Likewise Doug Leeby, now CEO of the HR technology firm Beeline, says he's never responded well whenever an outsider pushed a "best practice" on him. He would think, "You don't know my situation. You can't possibly call it a best practice until you really understand my context and the dynamics." For him, "the one that works best for you is the best practice."[6]

According to Pamela Hinds, professor of management science and engineering at Stanford, many leaders intuitively recognize that best practices come from success in a particular place and time "They're like a shoe that doesn't quite fit. You can put the shoe on, and it may even look nice, but it will likely create blisters if the fit isn't exactly right."[7] Hinds points to something as simple as how commute times can affect best practice adoption, in this case remote work technologies. Commutes to work in Mexico are much less predictable than in Japan. So working from home is more common there, and people more readily adopt virtual collaboration tools.

It's not just organizations that are becoming more unique; work itself is increasingly differentiated and, therefore, immune to best practice. According to the US Census Bureau, nonroutine work grew from 40% of occupations in 1975 to 60% in 2013 and is likely to encompass two-thirds of jobs by 2028.[8] Non-routine work tends to be cognitive versus manual and necessitates that people continually address new challenges and take on novel tasks. This work is hard to define; there are no manuals or precedent, making it much harder to identify or apply best practice.

Ronald Heifetz, founder of the Center for Public Leadership at Harvard Kennedy School and coauthor of *Leadership on the Line*, refers to this nonroutine work as an adaptive versus a technical challenge. Operating on a patient's heart is a technical challenge, because it uses similar procedures everywhere that can justly be deemed best practices. But getting that patient to change their lifestyle to reduce the risk of heart disease is an adaptive challenge because patients respond differently to various methods of persuasion.

Meanwhile, most best practices are outdated from the start. It usually takes quite a while for observers to recognize a successful practice. By the time other companies try it out, the world has changed.

Extending the 3M story, we can also see that the idea of best practice discourages learning and innovation. When leaders speak of "best," employees may feel obliged to accept them without question. Best practice creates a boundary around creativity; new perspectives or ideas are inevitably seen as inferior. Employees stop looking at edge cases, where creativity is likely to occur, and instead fall back on the status quo. The danger was described by the late C. K. Prahalad, professor at the University of Michigan, who wrote that best practice "may allow enterprises to catch up with competitors, but it won't turn them into market leaders. Organizations become winners by spotting big opportunities and identifying next practices."[9]

Take an example from publishing. J. K. Rowling's first Harry Potter novel got a dozen rejections, with the common response that the book was "far too long for children."[10] The best practice, in other words, was to publish children's books that weren't involved or taxing. Bloomsbury published the book almost by accident. Rowling's agent gave the small house a sample to read. Nigel Newton, the chairman of Bloomsbury, took it home, but rather than read it himself, he gave it to his eight-year-old daughter. An hour later she told him, "Dad, this is so much better than anything else," and nagged him for nine months to find out what came next. Even then, Newton offered only £2,500 for the book, which proved one of the wisest investments in publishing history.[11]

Despite these drawbacks, leaders struggle to give up the best-practice crutch. As described in Chapter 9, humans crave certainty. In the midst of uncertainty, our first reaction is often to find a solution—any solution—as quickly as possible. Moreover, during times of anxiety, we're apt to preserve energy, protect the status quo, and fall back on tried-and-true approaches.[12]

Best practices fit the bill. They're the "best," prescribed by experts. And coming up with your own ideas is hard. You risk pushback and ridicule.

There's comfort in conformity, as described by Mazher Ahmad, former chief learning officer for Regeneron: "If things don't work out, they can say 'Don't blame me. We used the best practice.'" Best practice becomes a crutch or cop out, and it encourages timidity at a time when leaders need to be aggressive and daring.[13]

Lou Gerstner deviated from best practice when he turned around IBM. In the early 1990s, the once great technology company faced multiple challenges and bankruptcy was a real possibility. The conventional wisdom was to break up the company so its individual units, the "Baby Blues," could better compete in their respective markets.

Gerstner, however, was the first outsider to lead IBM in 80 years. He didn't even come from tech. His experiences at American Express and RJR Nabisco led him to believe that IBM's true advantage was that it could provide customers with a broader, integrated package of hardware and services. He broke with the prevailing point of view, sustaining the company's core businesses while investing heavily in services.

Gerstner also took a much more customer-centric approach. When asked to attend a one-hour meeting with customers at an industry conference, he instead spent two full days with them and insisted other IBM executives do the same. He even disrupted IBM's storied white shirt culture, encouraging those with longer hair and earrings to join and even introducing humor into IBM's commercials. Ultimately, Gerstner's bold decisions saved and transformed IBM. During his tenure, the company's market value increased over 500%.[14]

Simplifying Complexity with Sensemaking

What enabled Gerstner to break with the prevailing views and established practice? How did he come up with his alternative approach and what gave him the confidence to pursue it? The answer is sensemaking, a way for leaders to act in the face of ambiguity.

First described by organizational theorist Karl Weick, sensemaking involves giving meaning to a challenging situation. MIT Sloan Professor Deborah Ancona identifies sensemaking as a critical leadership skill that enables action in the face of the unknown. Although problem-solving seeks to solve a known problem, sensemaking is about determining what problem to solve. It answers the questions, "What's going on here?" and "Why is it important?" and "What do we need to do about it?"

According to Ancona, sensemaking involves using intuition, experience, and logic to come up with "a plausible understanding—a map—of a shifting world; testing this map with others through data collection, action, and conversation; and then refining, or abandoning, the map depending on how credible it is."[15] Although Ancona refers to maps, other researchers use different terms—paradigms, mindsets, worldviews, cognitive lenses, and frames to describe the output of sensemaking. Whatever it's called, the output of sensemaking simplifies the complex and provides directional guidance. It enables leaders to relax, see more options, and move beyond established practice or the status quo.

Sensemaking is essentially theory building, coming up with a causal explanation for observations. Leaders in complex circumstances—shifting markets, changing regulations, disruptive technologies, and emerging rivals—must determine the relevant factors, define the relationships between them, develop hypotheses, test them to determine validity, and refine the theory accordingly. In this way, sensemaking—developing models or frameworks—is as much an act of creativity as it is an act of analysis. Leaders must choose where to focus their attention, what factors to consider, and how to represent their resulting mental map.

Markets have always had a good deal of uncertainty, and sensemaking has long been part of leadership. But in more stable business environments, leaders could outsource sensemaking. They could use models and frameworks that were developed elsewhere, apply best practices, and hire consultants with specific expertise to solve problems. Or they could rely on internal strategic planning departments far removed from the front lines, which often relied on external diagnoses anyway. In a volatile environment, every situation is unique, so leaders must participate in sensemaking themselves.

When Steve Jobs returned to take over a struggling Apple in 1997, the company was supporting 350 different products. Apple had spent millions of dollars and people hours building them and each one was "owned" by someone in the company. Although Jobs felt many of those products were pretty good, he believed Apple needed to be far more focused.

Jobs could have used a common, time-tested framework to determine which products to keep and which to jettison. Instead, he made sense of the situation for himself. He came up with a simple 2×2 matrix (consumer versus pro and desktop versus portable), and any product that didn't fit was gone, including the Newton, the Pippin, and 12 different versions of the Mac desktop.

Apple went from 350 products down to 10. It was a dramatic shift, but Jobs never wanted Apple to be just another computer company. The approach freed the company to develop its future hits, especially the iPhone, iTunes, and the app store.

Sensemaking is particularly necessary in unintelligible or unprecedented situations that require solutions outside of our usual routine. Think of Captain Chesley "Sully" Sullenberger landing a disabled Airbus 320 jet on New York's Hudson River in winter 2009. No pilot had ever experienced dual-engine failure at such a low altitude, much less over one of the world's most populated cities. There was simply no training for the scenario.

Despite the seemingly overwhelming circumstance, Sullenberger recognized he was no longer flying a commercial aircraft, he was piloting a 70-ton glider. Making sense of the situation in this new way enabled him to draw on his experience flying gliders in the US Air Force. He changed the aircraft's pitch to maintain optimal air speed, which provided the critical seconds needed for the plane to clear the George Washington Bridge and land safely on the river, saving all 155 passengers.

Leaders need to make sense of the changing world for colleagues, too. Groups that share an understanding of their environment can better act collectively. That's what the Chicago Cubs baseball team discovered in 2016.

At the time, the team hadn't won the championship in over a century. But the team's president of operations, Theo Epstein, was determined to change that and believed that the team had all the pieces in place except one—a strong collective identity. Everyone in the organization, from players to trainers, to front office personnel, had been asked what it means to be a Cub and nobody had a good answer.

"Historically, we were known as the 'Loveable Losers,'" said Josh Lifrak, director of the team's mental skills program. When people said, 'That's so Cub,' it was because someone made an error. We knew we had to co-opt the phrase; make it into something positive."[16]

The team turned Cub into an acronym that stood for "Courage to do the right thing, Urgency to do it right now, and Belief in reaching the top." And they used it to champion each other. As described by Lifrak, "When someone sprinted to first base even if they were out, we'd call it out and say 'Hey, that's so Cub,' when someone cleaned up the dugout after the game, we'd say 'That's so Cub,' or when someone was encouraging to another player we'd say, 'That's so Cub.' It became our identity and changed the way we operated."

The Cubs went on to beat the Cleveland Indians by one run in game seven of the 2016 World Series. "The cultural shift was a big part of winning the World Series," says Lifrak. "But it didn't just transform the team. It demonstrated to five million fans that anything is possible." Changing the organization's mindset unleased unexpected energies and discipline to persist to the top.

Although the goal of sensemaking, of course, is to build an accurate mental map of the situation, sensemaking has value for leaders and their teams even when the map is wrong. Karl Weick shares the story of a small military unit that got lost during a snowstorm in the Swiss Alps. The men were cold and hungry and had begun to panic. Then one of them found a map, which they used to navigate back to their base. Not surprisingly, the heavy snow made it hard to find some of the landmarks they anticipated, and they had to ask villagers for help along the way. It wasn't until they made it back safely that they realized they had been using a map of the Pyrenees rather than the Alps. The moral: in a crisis, any map, even the wrong one, is better than none, as long as people believe in it, because it enables us to act when the world feels inexplicable.[17]

Ultimately, in complex situations, sensemaking enables us to distill the complex: to build a map of the world around us so we can determine what's important and what to do about it. Additionally, sensemaking enables us to translate that understanding into simple terms so that everyone has a common understanding and can take action.

With best practices losing their credibility, leaders need to take back sensemaking for their organizations. As the complexity theorist W. Brian Arthur points out, "What distinguishes great leaders from average leaders is their ability to perceive the nature of the game and the rules by which it is played, as they are playing it."[18]

Scholars of complexity have long seen this challenge. Yes, despite research showing that sensemaking predicts leadership success, most executives don't even rate sensemaking as an important leadership attribute. Among the 1,395 traits or behaviors that executives link with great leadership, only a small portion (less than 4%) relate to sensemaking.[19] It's time for a renewed push for sensemaking in leadership.

Building Your Mental Map

By its very definition, sensemaking means acknowledging the unknown. So the first step is for leaders to accept vulnerability and embrace uncertainty (see Chapters 3 and 9). They have to plunge in despite the discomfort and anxiety this generates, both for themselves and their colleagues. And, they have to be courageous. Creating a new way of interpreting the world around you means challenging conventional wisdom. Those whose power is rooted in the status quo will push back.

Next, leaders must truly think creatively. As Weick notes, "Simply pushing harder within the old boundaries will not do."[20] Leaders must resist the human inclination to double down on what they already know. After all, if we want to change a system, we often have to be willing to look outside it for answers.

Part of this is understanding the boundaries that constrain our thinking. Imagine two colleagues are working feverishly to submit a proposal. They told their client when to expect it and promised their boss they'd get it done. But at some point, they realize they're not going to meet the deadline. As a result, they start debating what to cut out so they can finish on time. They might spend valuable time arguing about what to include and ultimately share an incomplete proposal when, in fact, the deadline itself was moveable. In this scenario, their underlying assumption about the need to submit the proposal "on time" prevented them from considering the possibility of asking for more time.

Additionally, leaders can ask questions such as "Why?" "How might we?" "What if?" "What would make this true?" "If not this, then what?" Asking questions helps gather and interpret information, clarify understanding, and identify knowledge gaps or assumptions. Through questioning, leaders can explore different perspectives and consider multiple angles to a problem, which enhances their ability to make sense of complex situations.

Leaders can also reason from first principles, foundational concepts or assumptions that cannot be further broken down or simplified. Reasoning from first principles involves breaking down a situation into its fundamental building blocks and then reassembling them from the ground up to improve understanding and generate new insight.

First-principles thinking was the basis for Elon Musk's decision to build his own rocket ships at SpaceX: He explained, "Physics teaches you to reason from first principles rather than by analogy. So I said, okay, let's look at the first principles. What is a rocket made of? Aerospace-grade aluminum alloys, plus some titanium, copper, and carbon fiber. Then I asked, what is the value of those materials on the commodity market? It turned out that the materials cost of a rocket was around two percent of the typical price."[21]

In his "Wait But Why" blog series on Musk, Tim Urban illustrates the point with the difference between a chef and a cook.[22] A chef possesses a deep understanding of gastronomy's first principles, which allows them to create new recipes and innovate in the kitchen. By contrast, a cook typically follows existing recipes, perhaps with some deviation, resulting in a dish that has been created countless times.

Leaders can also improve sensemaking by widening their aperture and considering the situation from different vantage points. A key principle of TRIZ, or the theory of inventive problem-solving, is the idea that someone, somewhere, likely came up with a solution for the challenge you currently face.[23] When people get stuck, they often look to experts in their field. Although these experts can help, they're likely to have a similar background and expertise and may therefore only confirm your existing assumptions. Sometimes it's better to expand your field of vision.

German housewife Melitta Bentz, for example, was frustrated by the grounds in her coffee and the effort required to clean linen filters. After experimenting with different potential solutions, she hit on the idea of using blotting paper from her son's school notebook. Designed to absorb excess ink, the paper was thicker and more absorbent, making it perfect for filtering coffee. In 1908, the Imperial Patent Office in Berlin granted her a patent. Today the Melitta Group employs close to 4,000 people worldwide and generates over $2 billion in revenue.[24]

Sensemaking is no lone heroic journey, however. As we've emphasized throughout this book, leaders are unwise to go it alone. They need to seek many different and diverse sources of data. They must speak with stakeholders from inside and outside the organization. Sensemaking isn't just about making sense for oneself. It's about creating shared meaning for the broader group. This requires conversation and interaction.

When Satya Nadella hosted his first executive retreat after becoming CEO of Microsoft, he arranged for vans to take everyone to customer sites so they could learn what was happening on the front lines. He also invited CEOs from recently acquired companies, who wouldn't ordinarily have been included in such senior meetings. These new additions had much to teach; after all, Microsoft had acquired their companies because they were at the forefront of new technologies and approaches. Both decisions sent the message that Nadella wanted his colleagues to work together to develop a deeper, more current map of what was happening in the marketplace.[25]

Escaping the Trap

Best practices are seductive, comforting, and reassuring in a time of great uncertainty. But they're often based on assumptions that are no longer relevant. The first is that leaders understand a problem well enough to know what the right best practice is. The second is that the same practices can be successfully applied in a different context. In today's complex world, neither is likely to be true.

Leaders must let go of the best practice safety net. Looking at what other organizations do to generate ideas is good, but insisting that others' practices are the "best" undermines creativity and adaptability and risks eroding trust.

As an alternative to best practices, leaders can use sensemaking to generate new insight and chart a differentiated path forward. Best practices are good for catching up with competitors, but companies that really want to get ahead need to come up with their own set of next practices.

12

Conclusion: The End of Leadership in a Quantum Age

As we write this book in early 2023, the business world is abuzz with the possibilities of artificial intelligence. Like the internet before it, ChatGPT and other generative AI approaches are creating unexpected opportunities and threats for many companies. Leaders are realizing they can't run their organizations as their predecessors did. It's time for a new approach.

But in case you aren't convinced of the need for change, let us tell you about quantum computing. In a decade or so, we're going to look back on conventional computing and marvel at its limitations. David Bryant, chief experience officer in IBM's quantum computing division, uses the analogy of finding a specific person, say, Dan Fisher, in a packed stadium. A conventional computer needs to check each person at a time, in effect, asking "Are you Dan Fisher, no . . . are you Dan Fisher, no . . . are you Dan Fisher?" If it's a stadium with 40,000 seats, on average, the conventional computer has to ask 20,000 people before it finds the actual Dan Fisher. A quantum computer uses a completely different approach. "It's like broadcasting over the stadium's jumbotron, 'Will Dan Fisher please stand up?' The quantum computer does it in just one step, not 20,000."[1]

The arrival of quantum computing will equip us to tackle problems that were previously unsolvable. You might think, for example, that we've made good progress in designing batteries. The truth is that we don't really understand how batteries work on the molecular level—fundamental battery technology has changed little in 50 years. With quantum computing, we'll finally be able to model and understand the inner workings of molecules, leading to batteries charged only once every six months, fertilizer that doesn't require fossil fuels, and dramatic new treatments for degenerative diseases. Quantum computers will also crack existing encryption protocols that keep our data safe. It's no wonder that governments are pouring billions into the technology and the industry has been described as the next "space race."

Quantum computing promises to bring ever more disruption and unpredictability to most every industry. But surely the most volatile and uncertain industry is quantum computing itself. IBM Quantum has more quantum computers than the rest of the world combined.[2] The division is a fascinating example of an adaptive organization that integrates new ways of leading with traditional big-company strengths.

Although IBM Quantum has some of the smartest people in the world, Bryant and other leaders aren't content with in-house expertise. They've built, and draw on, a dynamic network of cross-IBM and external relationships (Chapter 2). IBM's strong consulting relationships with business clients, for example, means that the quantum division can access internal aerospace expertise to help Boeing use quantum computing to develop new planes. The real-world challenge gives the team insight into applying quantum computing to solve real-world problems. In the same vein, the division's leaders decided early on to make the first quantum computers open to the public, so they put them on the cloud and educated people on how to use them for free. Now they have the largest network of quantum developers.

Part of that relational success comes from a willingness to be vulnerable (Chapter 3). The division's leaders chose to publicize their product road map, risking embarrassment if they missed target dates. The decision was a matter of internal debate, with some scientists arguing, "We don't talk about what we're planning to do, we talk about what we've done." But the vulnerability paid off. Other firms saw it as a sign of leadership, and IBM Quantum's road map now serves as a shared vision for companies across the industry.

Of course, given the complexity involved in building a quantum computer, the leaders know their road map will change. So they don't just strategize up front and then execute. Instead, as in a complex adaptive system, they continually sense and respond to their environment. "We're always open to new information," Bryant says. "There's an implicit understanding that things will change and when they do we stop, update the road map, and think about what we need to do differently to deliver on it." That's strategic doing (Chapter 4) at the divisional level.

Part of what enables the broader IBM Quantum team to orchestrate their efforts despite the unpredictable nature of their work are the clear purpose and simple rules that Bryant and others have established (Chapter 5). The internal mantra "Act like a startup, think like IBM" grounds the team and provides a standard for decisions and interactions. Within these guardrails, team members have the autonomy to decide for themselves how to organize and conduct their work. There is no single hero. It's a collaborative effort (Chapter 6).

That doesn't mean there isn't disagreement. Bryant will tell you that he and his colleagues are quick to share opposing views. But they're also steeped in rigorous science and can pivot when presented with new evidence. They don't resist change—they respond to it (Chapter 7). "It's a very passionate group. But the moment somebody else brings up some new information it's 'Oh, I didn't know that. Okay. I've changed my mind.'"

With so much uncertainty, teams at IBM Quantum avoid locking themselves into a single approach. Instead, they pursue multiple paths to learn what works best (Chapter 8). "We are forging ahead with different approaches and seeing which one wins, then pivoting hard on the winner."

This openness is driven by the teams' scientific background but also by a sense of wonder. They are, after all, on the vanguard of human knowledge, building something entirely new. Staying curious

(Chapter 9) instead of insisting on certainty or trying to impose order on an unpredictable environment increases their aperture and ability to discover.

Their openness to uncertainty also enables flexibility. In a division composed mostly of scientists, you'd expect leaders to depend heavily on data to make decisions. But in truth the science is highly intuitive (Chapter 10). Bryant notes, "While the actual process is very scientific and focused on the data, it's intuition that guides it, helping you figure out what to focus on and giving you strong indicators that something's going to work out or not."

Likewise, the IBM Quantum team can't rely on best practice. It simply doesn't exist on the leading edge. Instead, the team uses their own sensemaking abilities to figure things out (Chapter 11). Jay Gambetta, IBM's vice president of quantum, thinks like a physicist. "He thinks in terms of the variables, how they interact with each other, what's the equation?" says Bryant. Gambetta didn't apply an off-the-shelf model to design the IBM Quantum organization. He defined his own equation for the product's performance and built the team around it.

IBM Quantum is an extreme version of what we're seeing across industries in the broader economy. It's a huge change even from the economy of just a few decades ago when the internet first emerged. Waves of technological change have broken down industry boundaries, creating all sorts of unexpected capabilities. Quantum computing will do the same.

An End of Leadership . . . and a Beginning

This is the reality leaders increasingly face, and it's why we wrote this book. Business environments are changing faster and faster and moving in unexpected directions. Customer, supplier, and talent markets no longer fit in neat structures. As with the faraway student activist who pressures a company to settle a labor strike, leaders face new threats and opportunities that emerge from everywhere all at once.

To thrive in this near-chaotic space, leaders must model their organizations after complex adaptive systems. They must align the organization on simple rules, build out horizontal networks, decentralize decision-making, and conduct rapid test-and-learn cycles. This evolution, however, means that leaders need to show up and behave in new ways. They need to move from the sage on the stage to the guide on the side.

That's difficult, because few leaders rise to their position without strong egos. Once there, they tend to work from an established playbook that places leaders firmly at the center of the universe. But that playbook, created in the 20th century, is thoroughly outdated.

We've laid out the traps throughout the book that leaders must avoid as they evolve their organizations. They believe leadership stems from their own actions, not from relationships built with colleagues. They'd rather project confidence than show vulnerability. They craft strategy in advance and then tell everyone else what to do instead of working with others in rapid test-and-learn cycles. They don't appreciate the power of shared purpose to inspire and empower colleagues to work independently.

As problems arise, they'd rather be heroes who jump in to save the day, rather than reinforcers and accelerators who strengthen everyone else to overcome challenges. They're quick to steamroll colleagues who resist change, rather than treat that resistance as crucial feedback. They seek efficiency even at the cost of long-term resilience, and certainty at the cost of survival in the real world. They cling to data, giving information far more weight than it can bear, instead of courageously using their judgment. They privilege "best practices" that are ever less likely to fit the specifics of their situation.

It's validating to be the confident hero without vulnerabilities, to seek efficiency and certainty and rely on "proven" best practices and "hard" data, to pronounce grand strategies for others to implement, and to overcome resistance to change. It's all the more validating when those habits come with the imprimatur of success in previous decades. But these habits are driving companies off a cliff. What worked in the 20th century is failing now. In order to thrive, leaders need to build faster, more adaptive organizations. That means ending traditional leadership as we know it and developing a powerful, new set of practices.

Why We Feel Fine

Still, the validity of a new practice is never enough to guarantee adoption. Leaders must want to change. They need to see the advantage in it for their organizations, their customers, and themselves. It's a tall order—truly the end of leadership as we know it.

Yet we're optimistic about the future, for two reasons. First, as explained in Chapter 1, leaders have transformed their approaches in the past. The rise of systematic management in the early 20th century eventually forced leaders to shift from personal control to structured, organizational control. Then the rise of office work and the "human relations" movement prompted leaders to factor in knowledge workers and personnel dynamics. The spread of the multidivisional form capped off the century by creating highly structured bureaucracies, career ladders, and leadership development. What we know of as traditional leadership is only a few decades old. It changed before, and it will change again.

Second, and more important, we know that leaders don't just have strong egos; they also have strong ambition. They want to succeed and run organizations they can be proud of long after leaving, and they're pragmatic about how they get there. They see what happened to Jack Welch, who retired on top of the world, but left General Electric on a path of decline. Eventually, boards of directors will figure out what effective leadership takes and start selecting and promoting people according to how well they build adaptive organizations. Ambition will drive leaders to change how they operate.

Adaptation will also likely become the mantra of society in general. Just as the 20th century focused on achieving affluence through the disciplined employment of resources, the 21st century will be about connecting individual expression with larger communal and social needs. We need effective leaders more than ever. The ultimate goal of leadership is still to make groups of people more effective. So the end, or demise, of old leadership is just the beginning of a new kind of leadership that fits our current challenges.

Notes

Chapter 1

1. Kwoh, L. (2013, May 7). When the CEO burns out. *Wall Street Journal.* https://www.wsj.com/articles/SB10001424127887323687604578469124008524696
2. McKinsey & Company. (2017, January 10). ING's agile transformation. *McKinsey Quarterly.* https://www.mckinsey.com/industries/financial-services/our-insights/ings-agile-transformation
3. Harwell, D. (2021, December 16). A Reddit "antiwork" mob is fighting back. *Washington Post.* https://www.washingtonpost.com/technology/2021/12/16/reddit-kellogg-strike-antiwork/
4. Charette, R. N. (2013, September 4). An engineering career: Only a young person's game? IEEE Spectrum. https://spectrum.ieee.org/an-engineering-career-only-a-young-persons-game
5. Sull, D., Homkes, R., & Sull, C. (2015, March). Why strategy execution unravels—and what to do about it. *Harvard Business Review*, https://hbr.org/2015/03/why-strategy-execution-unravelsand-what-to-do-about-it
6. Authors' interview with DeLisa Alexander, Sept. 2, 2022.
7. Bergen, P. (2023, February 14). Gen. David Petraeus: How the war in Ukraine will end. CNN. https://www.cnn.com/2023/02/14/opinions/petraeus-how-ukraine-war-ends-bergen-ctpr/index.html
8. Ackerman, E. (2022, March 24). Ukraine's three-to-one advantage. *The Atlantic.* https://www.theatlantic.com/ideas/archive/2022/03/american-volunteer-foreign-fighters-ukraine-russia-war/627604/

9. Fidler, S., & Michaels, D. (2023, January 3). Russia's basic errors jeopardize its Ukraine forces, military analysts say. *Wall Street Journal*. https://www.wsj.com/articles/russias-repeated-errors-jeopardize-its-ukraine-forces-military-analysts-say-11672774752

10. Fidler, S., Marson, J., & Grove, T. (2022, October 12). How Ukrainian strategy is running circles around Russia's lumbering military. *Wall Street Journal*. https://www.wsj.com/articles/how-ukraines-strategy-is-running-circles-around-russias-lumbering-military-11665584517

11. Dickinson, P. (2022, December 19). 2022 review: Why has Vladimir Putin's Ukraine invasion gone so badly wrong. Atlantic Council. https://www.atlanticcouncil.org/blogs/ukrainealert/2022-review-why-has-vladimir-putins-ukraine-invasion-gone-so-badly-wrong/

Chapter 2

1. Authors' interview with Ivan Berg, Nov. 4, 2022

2. Groysberg, B., Nanda, A., & Nohria, N. (2004, May). The risky business of hiring stars. *Harvard Business Review*. https://hbr.org/2004/05/the-risky-business-of-hiring-stars

3. Goldsmith, M., & Morgan, H. (2004, August 25). Leadership is a contact sport: The "follow-up factor" in management development. *Strategy + Business*. https://www.strategy-business.com/article/04307?pg=0

4. Friedrich, T. L., Vessey, W. B., Schuelke, M. J., Ruark, G. A., & Mumford, M. D. (2011). *A framework for understanding collective leadership: The selective utilization of leader and team expertise within networks.* United States Army Research Institute for the Behavioral and Social Sciences.

5. Gladwell, M. (2002). *The tipping point.* Back Bay Books.

6. Burt, R. S. (2005). Structural holes and good ideas. *American Journal of Sociology, 110*(2), 349–399.

7. Bigda-Peyton, T., Rabinowitz, J., Schloss, S., & Theilmann, M. (2021, May 14). Panel discussion. In Garcia, S. (Chair), Organizational transformation amidst the Covid-19 pandemic. Institution for Contemporary Leadership Webinar.

8. Hill, S., & Bartol, K. (2015, March). Empowering leadership and effective collaboration in geographically dispersed teams. *Personnel Psychology*. https://onlinelibrary.wiley.com/doi/abs/10.1111/peps.12108

9. Fowler, J. H., & Christakis, N. A. (2009). *Connected: The surprising power of our social networks and how they shape our lives.* Little, Brown and Co.
10. Moeller, P. (2012, March 16). How to find happiness on social networks. *U.S. News & World Report.* https://money.usnews.com/money/personal-finance/articles/2012/03/16/how-to-find-happiness-on-social-networks
11. Thompson, B. (2022). How Leaders Develop Collaborative Leadership for Effectiveness. *Dissertations available from ProQuest.* AAI28964056. https://repository.upenn.edu/dissertations/AAI28964056
12. Garcia, S., & O'Driscoll, T. (2020). Networks not hierarchy: Expanding leadership capacity and impact in a complex world. The Institute for Contemporary Leadership. https://contemporaryleadership.com/network-leadership/
13. Authors' interview with Tom Bigda-Peyton, August 31, 2022.
14. Cuddy, A., Kohut, M., & Neffinger, J. (2013, July–March). Connect, then lead. *Harvard Business Review.* https://hbr.org/2013/07/connect-then-lead
15. Thomas, D. A. (2001, April). Race matters. *Harvard Business Review.* https://hbr.org/2001/04/race-matters
16. Dunbar, R. (2021, May 12). Dunbar's number: Why my theory that humans can only maintain 150 friendships has withstood 30 years of scrutiny. The Conversation. https://theconversation.com/dunbars-number-why-my-theory-that-humans-can-only-maintain-150-friendships-has-withstood-30-years-of-scrutiny-160676
17. Cross, R., & Thomas, R. J. (2011, July–August). Managing yourself: A smarter way to network. *Harvard Business Review.* https://hbr.org/2011/07/managing-yourself-a-smarter-way-to-network

Chapter 3

1. Chrobot-Mason, D., Ernst, C., & Ferguson, J. (2014). *Boundary spanning as battle rhythm.* Center for Creative Leadership.
2. Brown, B. (2018). *Dare to lead: Brave work. Tough conversations. Whole hearts.* Random House.
3. Howe, L. C., Menges, J. I., & Monks, J. (2021, August 21). Leaders, don't be afraid to talk about your fears and anxieties. *Harvard Business*

Review. https://hbr.org/2021/08/leaders-dont-be-afraid-to-talk-about-your-fears-and-anxieties

4. le Gentil, H. (2021, October 25). Leaders, stop trying to be heroes. *Harvard Business Review.* https://hbr.org/2021/10/leaders-stop-trying-to-be-heroes

5. Viguerie, S. P., Calder, N., & Hindo, B. (2021, May). 2021 corporate longevity forecast. Innosight. https://www.innosight.com/insight/creative-destruction/

6. Bort, J. (2015, June 8). Retiring Cisco CEO delivers dire prediction: 40% of companies will be dead in 10 years. *Business Insider.* https://www.businessinsider.com/chambers-40-of-companies-are-dying-2015-6

7. Porter, T., Elnakouri, A., Meyers, F. A., et al. (2022). Predictors and consequences of intellectual humility. *Nature Reviews Psychology, 1,* 524–536. https://doi.org/10.1038/s44159-022-00081-9

8. Dweck, C. S. (2006). *Mindset: The new psychology of success.* Random House.

9. Authors' interview with David Chang, June 30, 2022.

10. Cable, D. (2022, July 14). How to build confidence about showing vulnerability. *Harvard Business Review.* https://hbr.org/2022/07/how-to-build-confidence-about-showing-vulnerability

11. Restrepo, S. (Director). (2019). *Brené Brown: The call to courage* [Motion Picture].

12. Coyle, D. (2018, February 20). How showing vulnerability helps build a stronger team. Ideas.Ted.Com. https://ideas.ted.com/how-showing-vulnerability-helps-build-a-stronger-team/

13. Eadeh, F., Ostrowski, B., & Woolley, A. W. (2021). Misery loves company: The implications of mood for affiliation and collective intelligence in remote collaboration. Presented at the Interdisciplinary Network for Group Research (INGRoup) Virtual Conference, October.

14. Seppala, E. (2014, December 11). What bosses gain by being vulnerable. *Harvard Business Review.* https://hbr.org/2014/12/what-bosses-gain-by-being-vulnerable

15. Butler, E. A., Egloff, B., Wlhelm, F. H., Smith, N. C., Erickson, E. A., & Gross, J. J. (2003). The social consequences of expressive suppression. *Emotion, 3*(1), 48–67. https://doi.org/10.1037/1528-3542.3.1.48

16. Jones, R. (2015, February 24). What CEOs are afraid of. *Harvard Business Review.* https://hbr.org/2015/02/what-ceos-are-afraid-of

17. Sherman, A. (2021, December 21). Disney chairman Bob Iger explains why he's leaving the company and how he acquired Pixar, Lucasfilm and Marvel. CNBC. https://www.cnbc.com/2021/12/21/disney-chairman-bob-iger-explains-why-hes-leaving-the-company.html
18. Argyris, C. (1991, May–June). Teaching smart people how to learn. *Harvard Business Review*. https://hbr.org/1991/05/teaching-smart-people-how-to-learn
19. Inc. (2020, June 18). Simon Sinek on how to show vulnerability as a leader. *Inc*. https://www.inc.com/video/simon-sinek-how-to-show-vulnerability-as-a-leader.html
20. Chelsea Mitamura, personal communication with authors, January 13, 2022.
21. Nair, L. (2021, December 9). The soft stuff is the hard stuff: Leaders must show vulnerability in uncertain times. *Fortune*. https://fortune.com/2021/12/05/leaders-must-show-vulnerability-in-uncertain-times-hr-leadership-pandemic-grief-workplace-leena-nair-unilever/
22. Cohn, J., & Rangan, R. S. (2020, May 11). Why CEOs should model vulnerability. *Harvard Business Review*. https://hbr.org/2020/05/why-ceos-should-model-vulnerability
23. Seppala, E., & Bradley, C. (2019, June 11). Handling negative emotions in a way that's good for your team. *Harvard Business Review*. https://hbr.org/2019/06/handling-negative-emotions-in-a-way-thats-good-for-your-team
24. Howe, L. C., Menges, J. I., & Monks, J. (2021, August 21). Leaders, don't be afraid to talk about your fears and anxieties. *Harvard Business Review*. https://hbr.org/2021/08/leaders-dont-be-afraid-to-talk-about-your-fears-and-anxieties
25. Schweitzer, M., Brooks, A. W., & Galinsky, A. (2015, September). The organizational apology. *Harvard Business Review*. https://hbr.org/2015/09/the-organizational-apology
26. Shopsin, T. (2015, June 1). To be sued less, doctors should consider talking to patients more. *New York Times*. https://www.nytimes.com/2015/06/02/upshot/to-be-sued-less-doctors-should-talk-to-patients-more.html

Chapter 4

1. Bigda-Peyton, T., Rabinowitz, J., Schloss, S., & Theilmann, M. (2021, May 14). Panel discussion. In Garcia, S. (Chair), Organizational transformation amidst the Covid-19 pandemic. Institution for Contemporary Leadership Webinar.

2. Sull, D., Homkes, R., & Sull, C. (2015, March). Why strategy execution unravels—and what to do about it. *Harvard Business Review*. https://hbr.org/2015/03/why-strategy-execution-unravelsand-what-to-do-about-it

3. Avishai, B. (2020). The pandemic isn't a black swan but a portent of a more fragile global system. *The New Yorker*. https://www.newyorker.com/news/daily-comment/the-pandemic-isnt-a-black-swan-but-a-portent-of-a-more-fragile-global-system

4. Sull, D., Homkes, R., & Sull, C. (2015, March). Why strategy execution unravels—and what to do about it. *Harvard Business Review*. https://hbr.org/2015/03/why-strategy-execution-unravelsand-what-to-do-about-it

5. Reynolds, A., & Lewis, D. (2017, October 30). Closing the strategy-execution gap means focusing on what employees think, not what they do. *Harvard Business Review*. https://hbr.org/2017/10/closing-the-strategy-execution-gap-means-focusing-on-what-employees-think-not-what-they-do

6. Cappelli, P., & Eldor, L. (2019, May 17). Where measuring engagement goes wrong. *Harvard Business Review*. https://hbr.org/2019/05/where-measuring-engagement-goes-wrong

7. Kaplan, S. (2021, Dec. 16). Don't create a plan. Create a strategy uncertainty map. *Inc*. https://www.inc.com/soren-kaplan/dont-create-a-plan-create-a-strategy-uncertainty-map.html

8. Lupica, M. (1988, Feb. 1). The brawling existentialist. *Esquire*. https://classic.esquire.com/article/1988/2/1/the-brawling-existentialist

9. Bhide, A. (2000). *The origin and evolution of new businesses*. Oxford University Press.

10. Martin, R. (2017, April 3). Strategic choices need to be made simultaneously, not sequentially. *Harvard Business Review*. https://hbr.org/2017/04/strategic-choices-need-to-be-made-simultaneously-not-sequentially

11. Kostov, N. (2023, January 7). The executive who made winter gear high fashion. *Wall Street Journal.* https://www.wsj.com/articles/the-executive-who-made-winter-gear-high-fashion-11673032917

12. Martin, R. L. (2014, January–February). The big lie of strategic planning. *Harvard Business Review.* https://hbr.org/2014/01/the-big-lie-of-strategic-planning

13. Stewart, T. A., & Raman, A. P. (2007, July–August). Lessons from Toyota's long drive. *Harvard Business Review.* https://hbr.org/2007/07/lessons-from-toyotas-long-drive; and Takeuchi, H., Oono, E., & Shimizu, N. (2008, June). The contradictions that drive Toyota's success. *Harvard Business Review.* https://hbr.org/2008/06/the-contradictions-that-drive-toyotas-success

14. Catmull, E. (2008, September). How Pixar fosters collective creativity. *Harvard Business Review.* https://hbr.org/2008/09/how-pixar-fosters-collective-creativity

15. Clifford, C. (2017, June 5). How Mark Zuckerberg keeps Facebook's 18,000+ employees innovating: "Is this going to destroy the company? If not, let them test it." CNBC. https://www.cnbc.com/2017/06/05/how-mark-zuckerberg-keeps-facebook-employees-innovating.html

16. Clark, B. (2016, September 21). Why these tech companies keep running thousands of failed experiments. Fast Company. Retrieved from: https://www.fastcompany.com/3063846/why-these-tech-companies-keep-running-thousands-of-failed

Chapter 5

1. Business Roundtable. (2019, August 2019). Business Roundtable Redefines the purpose of a corporation to promote "an economy that serves all Americans." https://www.businessroundtable.org/business-roundtable-redefines-the-purpose-of-a-corporation-to-promote-an-economy-that-serves-all-americans

2. Harvard Business Review Analytic Services. (2015). The business case for purpose. *Harvard Business Review.*

3. Gartenberg, C. M., Prat, A., & Serafeim, G. (2016). Corporate purpose and financial performance. *Columbia Business School Research Paper No. 16-69,* https://repository.upenn.edu/mgmt_papers/274

4. Gulati, R. (2022, March–April). The messy but essential pursuit of purpose. *Harvard Business Review.* https://hbr.org/2022/03/the-messy-but-essential-pursuit-of-purpose

5. Authors' interview with Alexander, 2022.

6. The Business Case for Purpose (2015).

7. Carucci, R., & Ridge, G. (2022, November 3). How executive teams shape a company's purpose. *Harvard Business Review.* https://hbr.org/2022/11/how-executive-teams-shape-a-companys-purpose

8. Eisenhardt, K. M., & Sull, D. (2001, January). Strategy as simple rules. *Harvard Business Review.* https://hbr.org/2001/01/strategy-as-simple-rules

9. McGregor, J. (2016, December 8). Brick by brick: The man who rebuilt the house of Lego shares his leadership secrets. *Washington Post.* https://www.washingtonpost.com/news/on-leadership/wp/2016/12/08/brick-by-brick-the-man-who-rebuilt-the-house-of-lego-shares-his-leadership-secrets/

10. Alexander, A. K., & Douthit, M. W. (2017, November 30). The power of purpose: How organizations are making work more meaningful. *Academy of Management.* https://journals.aom.org/doi/10.5465/ambpp.2016.11489abstract

11. How Executive Teams Shape a Company's Purpose. (2022, November 3).

12. Edelman. (2022). Edelman Trust Barometer 2022. https://www.edelman.com/trust/2022-trust-barometer

13. Ives, N. (2021, May 6). Consumers are more likely to use or drop brands based on racial justice response, survey finds. *Wall Street Journal.* https://www.wsj.com/articles/consumers-are-more-likely-to-use-or-drop-brands-based-on-racial-justice-response-survey-finds-11620333257

14. Avila, M., Parkin, H., & Galoostian, S. (2019). $16.7 million to save one reputation: How Starbucks responded amidst a racial sensitivity crisis. *Pepperdine Journal of Communication Research, 7*(Article 4). https://digitalcommons.pepperdine.edu/pjcr/vol7/iss1/4/

15. Leinwand, P., & Rotering, J. (2017, November 17). How to excel at both strategy and execution. *Harvard Business Review.* https://hbr.org/2017/11/how-to-excel-at-both-strategy-and-execution

16. Quinn, R. E., & Thakor, A. V. (2018, July–August). Creating a purpose-driven organization. *Harvard Business Review.* https://hbr.org/2018/07/creating-a-purpose-driven-organization

17. Gulati, R. (2022). *Deep purpose: The heart and soul of high-performance companies.* HarperCollins.
18. Nonaka, I., & Takeuchi, H. (2021). Strategy as a way of life. *MIT Sloan Management Review.* https://sloanreview.mit.edu/article/strategy-as-a-way-of-life/
19. Gast, A., Illanes, P., Probst, N., Schaninger, B., & Simpson, B. (2020, April 22). Purpose: Shifting from why to how. *McKinsey Quarterly.* https://www.mckinsey.com.br/capabilities/people-and-organizational-performance/our-insights/purpose-shifting-from-why-to-how
20. Authors' interview with Ray Hill, August 25, 2022.
21. Authors' interview with Garry Ridge, August 30, 2022.

Chapter 6

1. Insights from Dr. Patrick O'Shaughnessy. (2023, February 5). Catholic Health. https://www.chsli.org/patrick-oshaughnessy-2/insights; Authors' interview with Tom Bigda-Peyton, August 31, 2022.
2. Graef, C. (1991). *In search of excess: The overcompensation of American executives.* Norton.
3. Auletta, K. (2014, December 8). Blood, simpler. *The New Yorker.* https://www.newyorker.com/magazine/2014/12/15/blood-simpler
4. Sing, M. (2022, July 14). The "shamanification" of the tech CEO. *Wired.* https://www.wired.com/story/health-business-deprivation-technology/
5. Authors' interview with DeLisa Alexander, September 2, 2022.
6. Mintzberg, H. (2009, July–August). Rebuilding companies as communities. *Harvard Business Review.* https://hbr.org/2009/07/rebuilding-companies-as-communities
7. Owen, D., & Davidson, J. (2009). Hubris syndrome: An acquired personality disorder? A study of US presidents and UK prime ministers over the last 100 years. *Brain, 132*(5), 396–1406. https://doi.org/10.1093/brain/awp008
8. Hougaard, R., & Carter, J. (2016, November 6). Ego is the enemy of good leadership. *Harvard Business Review.* https://hbr.org/2018/11/ego-is-the-enemy-of-good-leadership
9. Hy, L. X., & Loevinger, J. (2014). *Measuring ego development.* Psychology Press.

10. Schwantes, M. (2017, April 6). 20 leadership quotes by successful women you should pay attention to. *Inc.* https://www.inc.com/marcel-schwantes/20-leadership-quotes-by-successful-female-entrepreneurs-that-will-make-you-jealo.html

11. De Vita, E. (2019, March 6). Reverse mentoring: What young women can teach the old guard. *Financial Times.* https://www.ft.com/content/53d12284-391f-11e9-b856-5404d3811663

12. Badal, S. B., & Ott, B. (2015, April 14). Delegating: A huge management challenge for entrepreneurs. Gallup. https://news.gallup.com/businessjournal/182414/delegating-huge-management-challenge-entrepreneurs.aspx

13. Fredberg, T. (2011, October 6). Why good leaders pass the credit and take the blame. *Harvard Business Review.* https://hbr.org/2011/10/why-good-leaders-pass-the-cred#:~:text=A%20leader%20who%20spreads%20the,the%20collective%20enterprise%20to%20flourish

14. Satterstrom, P., Kerrissey, M., & DiBenigno, J. (2021). The voice cultivation process: How team members can help upward voice live on to implementation. *Administrative Science Quarterly, 66*(2), 380–425. https://doi.org/10.1177/0001839220962795

15. Bain, K., Kreps, T. A., Meikle, N. L., & Tenney, E. R. (2021, June 17). Research: Amplifying your colleagues' voices benefits everyone. *Harvard Business Review.* https://hbr.org/2021/06/research-amplifying-your-colleagues-voices-benefits-everyone

16. Dickinson, P. (2022, December 19). 2022 review: Why has Vladimir Putin's Ukraine invasion gone so badly wrong? Atlantic Council. https://www.atlanticcouncil.org/blogs/ukrainealert/2022-review-why-has-vladimir-putins-ukraine-invasion-gone-so-badly-wrong/

17. Authors' interview with Amy Hanlon-Rodemich, September 15, 2022.

18. Hofstede, G. (1980). *Culture's consequences: International differences in work-related values.* SAGE.

Chapter 7

1. Allison, C. (2014, February 10). The responsive organization: Coping with new technology and disruption. Retrieved from https://www.forbes.com/sites/scottallison/2014/02/10/the-responsive-organization-how-to-cope-with-technology-and-disruption/?sh=6924c6123cdd

2. Machiavelli, N., & Bull, G. (2003). *The prince*. Penguin Classics.
3. Porras, J. I., & Robertson, P. J. (1983). Organization development: Theory, practice, and research. In M. D. Dunnette & L. M. Hough (Eds.), *The handbook of industrial and organizational psychology* (Vol. 3, pp. 719–822). Consulting Psychologists Press.
4. Beer, M., Eisenstat, R. A., & Spector, B. (1990). Why change programs do not produce change. *Harvard Business Review, 68*(6), 158–166.
5. Ewenstein, B., Smith, W., & Sologar, A. (2015, July 1). Changing change management. McKinsey. https://www.mckinsey.com/featured-insights/leadership/changing-change-management
6. Cahill, J. (2020, July 21). The Brightline Initiative—helping organizations transform. Project Management Institute. https://www.pmi.org/learning/training-development/center-stage-podcast/podcasts/the-brightline-initiative---helping-organizations-transform
7. Freud, S. (1989). Beyond the pleasure principle. In P. Gay, *The Freud reader* (pp. 612–613). W. W. Norton & Co.
8. Spreitzer, G., & Quinn, R. (1996). Empowering middle managers to be transformational leaders. *Journal of Applied Behavioral Science, 32*. 10.1177/0021886396323001.
9. Teuscher, C. (2022). Revisiting the edge of chaos: Again? *Biosystems, 218*. https://doi.org/10.1016/j.biosystems.2022.104693
10. Kauffman, S. (1995). *At home in the universe: The search for the laws of self-organization and complexity*. Oxford University Press.
11. Wheatley, M. J., & Kellner-Rogers, M. (1998, April/May). Bringing life to organizational change. https://www.margaretwheatley.com/articles/life.html
12. Authors' interview with Michael Arena, February 17, 2022.
13. Authors' interview with Michael Arena, February 17, 2022.
14. Acar, O. A., Tarakci, M., & van Knippenberg, D. (2019, November 22). Why constraints are good for innovation. *Harvard Business Review*. https://hbr.org/2019/11/why-constraints-are-good-for-innovation

Chapter 8

1. Martin, R. L. (2019, January–February). The high price of efficiency. *Harvard Business Review*. https://hbr.org/2019/01/the-high-price-of-efficiency

2. Andriani, P., & McKelvey, B. (2011). Managing in a pareto world calls for new thinking. *M@n@gement*, 14(2). doi:10.3917/mana.142.0089. Note that consumers and workers received the bulk of rewards from efficiency during most of the decades of capitalism. Only in the early 20th century and recently has efficiency increased, rather than decreased, income inequality.

3. Grullon, G., Larkin, Y., & Michaely, R. (2019). Are US industries becoming more consolidated? *Review of Finance*, 23(4), 697–743.

4. Piketty, T. (2017). *Capital in the twenty-first century*. The Belknap Press of Harvard University Press.

5. Grullon, G., Larkin, Y., & Michaely, R. (2019) Are US industries becoming more consolidated? *Review of Finance*, 23(4), 697–743.

6. Galston, W. A. (2020, March 10). Efficiency isn't the only economic virtue. *Wall Street Journal*. https://www.wsj.com/articles/efficiency-isnt-the-only-economic-virtue-11583873155

7. Perrow, C. (1984). *Normal accidents: Living with high-risk technologies*. Basic Books.

8. Hamel, G., & Valikangas, L. (2003, September). The quest for resilience. *Harvard Business Review*. https://hbr.org/2003/09/the-quest-for-resilience

9. Reeves, M., Levin, S., Desai, S., & Whitaker, K. (2020). Resilience vs. efficiency: Calibrating the tradeoff. BCG Henderson Institute. https://bcghendersoninstitute.com/resilience-vs-efficiency-calibrating-the-tradeoff/#:~:text=Resilience%20vs.-,Efficiency%3A%20Calibrating%20the%20Tradeoff,tradeoffs%20between%20resilience%20and%20efficiency

10. Reeves, M., Nanda, S., Whitaker, K., & Wesselink, E. (2020, September 9). Becoming an all-weather company. BCG Henderson Institute. https://www.bcg.com/publications/2020/how-to-become-an-all-weather-resilient-company

11. Leary, W. E. (1995, September 24). Congress' science agency prepares to close its doors. *New York Times*. https://www.nytimes.com/1995/09/24/us/congress-s-science-agency-prepares-to-close-its-doors.html

12. Kennedy, P. (2012, January 13). William Gibson's future is now. *New York Times*. https://www.nytimes.com/2012/01/15/books/review/distrust-that-particular-flavor-by-william-gibson-book-review.html#:~:

text=%E2%80%9CThe%20future%20is%20already%20here,up%20
his%20own%20particular%20flavor

13. Thomas, K. (2020, July 9). These scientists raced to find a Covid-19 drug. Then the virus found them. *New York Times.* https://www.nytimes.com/2020/07/09/health/regeneron-monoclonal-antibodies.html

14. Summary of "lessons learned" from events of September 11 and implications for business continuity. (2002, February 13). Securities and Exchange Commission. https://www.sec.gov/divisions/marketreg/lessonslearned.htm

15. Irving, Z. C., McGrath, C., Flynn, L., Glasser, A., & Mills, C. (2022). The shower effect: Mind wandering facilitates creative incubation during moderately engaging activities. *Psychology of Aesthetics, Creativity, and the Arts,* Advance online publication. https://doi.org/10.1037/aca0000516

16. Gross, J. (2022, September 22). 4-day workweek brings no loss of productivity, companies in experiment say. *New York Times.* https://www.nytimes.com/2022/09/22/business/four-day-work-week-uk.html?searchResultPosition=7

17. Hamel, G., & Valikangas, L. (2003, September). The quest for resilience. *Harvard Business Review.* https://hbr.org/2003/09/the-quest-for-resilience

18. Authors' interview with Ginger Miller, August 3, 2022.

19. Cross, R., Benson, M., Kostal, J., & Milnor, R. J. (2021, September 7). Collaboration overload is sinking productivity. *Harvard Business Review.* https://hbr.org/2021/09/collaboration-overload-is-sinking-productivity

Chapter 9

1. Doyle, A. C. (1894). *The Memoirs of Sherlock Holmes.* George Newnes. Note that Batman is clearly the world's greatest fictional detective.

2. Schaefer, M. (2018). *The certainty of uncertainty.* Wipf & Stock.

3. Blodget, H. (2010, June 30). Flashback: Steve Ballmer's first take on the iPhone, January 2007. *Business Insider.* https://www.businessinsider.com/flashback-steve-ballmers-first-take-on-the-iphone-september-22-2007-2010-6

4. Catmull, E. (2008, September). How Pixar fosters collective creativity. *Harvard Business Review.* https://hbr.org/2008/09/how-pixar-fosters-collective-creativity

5. Gino, F. (2018, October). The business case for curiosity. *Harvard Business Review.* https://hbr.org/2018/09/the-business-case-for-curiosity

6. Gino. (2018, October).

7. Authors' interview with Ray Hill, August 25, 2022.

8. Chu, L., Tsai, J. L., & Fung, H. H. (2021). Association between age and intellectual curiosity: The mediating roles of future time perspective and importance of curiosity. *European Journal of Ageing, 18*(1), 45–53.

9. Gino. (2018, October).

10. Authors' interview with Ray Hill, August 25, 2022.

11. Calaprice, A. (2011). *The ultimate quotable Einstein.* Princeton University Press.

12. Drake, A., Dore, B. P., Falk, E. B., Zurn, P., Bassett, D. S., & Lydon-Staley, D. M. (2022). Daily stressor-related negative mood and its associations with flourishing and daily curiosity. *Journal of Happiness Studies, 23.* 423–438. https://10.1007/s10902-021-00404-2

13. Costa, V. D., Tran, V. L., Turchi, J., & Averbeck, B. B. (2014). Dopamine modulates novelty seeking behavior during decision making. *Behavioral Neuroscience, 128*(5), 556–566. https://doi.org/10.1037/a0037128

14. Tormala, Z. L., & Rucker, D. D. (2016, November 16). The upside of uncertainty. *Scientific American.* https://www.scientificamerican.com/article/the-upside-of-uncertainty/

15. Fernández-Araoz, C., Roscoe, A., & Aramaki, K. (2018). From curious to competent: How to move your people up the learning curve. *Harvard Business Review.* https://hbr.org/2018/09/from-curious-to-competent

16. Sloan, A. (1963). *My years with General Motors.* Doubleday.

17. Brendel, D. (2017, September 17). Asking open-ended questions helps new managers build trust. *Harvard Business Review.* https://hbr.org/2015/09/asking-open-ended-questions-helps-new-managers-build-trust

18. Brooks, A. W., & John, L. K. (2018, May–June). The surprising power of questions. *Harvard Business Review.* https://hbr.org/2018/05/the-surprising-power-of-questions

19. Brooks & John. (2018, May-June).

20. Brody, L. (2022, Jan. 1). Meet the elite team of superforecasters who have turned future-gazing into a science. *Entrepreneur*. https://www.entrepreneur.com/growing-a-business/meet-the-elite-team-of-superforecasters-who-have-turned/395236
21. Tetlock, P. E., & Gardner, D. (2015). *Superforecasting: The art and science of prediction*. Broadway Books.

Chapter 10

1. Fox, J. (2014, June 20). Instinct can beat analytical thinking. *Harvard Business Review*. https://hbr.org/2014/06/instinct-can-beat-analytical-thinking
2. Mark Zuckerberg now puts Meta's middle managers on notice. (2023, January 30). *The Economic Times*. https://economictimes.indiatimes.com/tech/technology/mark-zuckerberg-now-puts-metas-middle-managers-on-notice/articleshow/97434034.cms
3. Kantrowitz, A. (2022, November 21). The bad bet tech companies made that got them into this mess. *Slate*. https://slate.com/technology/2022/11/meta-amazon-shopify-tech-layoffs-pandemic.html
4. Press, A. N. (2021, December 17). The hellish reality of Amazon's human resource department. Jacobin. https://jacobin.com/2021/12/amazon-human-resources-department-mental-health-upt
5. Johnson, E. (2019, June 26). The problem with tech people who want to solve problems. Vox. https://www.vox.com/recode/2019/6/26/18758776/joi-ito-mit-media-lab-resisting-reduction-exorcist-kara-swisher-recode-decode-podcast-interview
6. Ryan, J. (2022, November 20). Meta trained an AI on 48m science papers. It was shut down after 2 days. *CNET*. https://www.cnet.com/science/meta-trained-an-ai-on-48-million-science-papers-it-was-shut-down-after-two-days/
7. Shah, S., Horne, A., & Capella, J. (2012). Good data won't guarantee good decisions. *Harvard Business Review*. https://hbr.org/2012/04/good-data-wont-guarantee-good-decisions
8. Hayashi, A. M. (2001, February). When to trust your gut. *Harvard Business Review*. https://hbr.org/2001/02/when-to-trust-your-gut

9. Sull, D., & Eisenhardt, K. M. (2012, September). Simple rules for a complex world. *Harvard Business Review.* https://hbr.org/2012/09/simple-rules-for-a-complex-world

10. Authors' interview with Rose Else-Mitchell, August 1, 2022.

11. Samples, B. (1976). *The metaphoric mind: A celebration of creative consciousness.* Addison-Wesley.

12. Patel, N. (2021, December 21). How Logitech bet big on work from home. The Verge. https://www.theverge.com/22846681/logitech-ceo-interview-mouse-keyboard-work-from-home-pc-g502-decoder-podcast

13. Hayashi, A. M. (2001, February). When to trust your gut. *Harvard Business Review.* https://hbr.org/2001/02/when-to-trust-your-gut

14. Hayashi. (2001, February).

15. Gaudiano, P. (2017, June 20). The best approach to decision making combines data and manager' expertise. *Harvard Business Review.* https://hbr.org/2017/06/the-best-approach-to-decision-making-combines-data-and-managers-expertise

16. Shah, Horne, & Capella. (2012, April).

17. Amazon. (2015). Letter to shareholders. https://www.aboutamazon.com/news/company-news/2015-letter-to-shareholders

18. Snowden, D. J., & Boone, M. E. (2007, November). A leader's framework for decision making. *Harvard Business Review.* https://hbr.org/2007/11/a-leaders-framework-for-decision-making

19. Authors' interview with David Chang, July 6, 2022.

20. Robinson, J., & Beaton, A. (2021, December 10). Computers revolutionized chess. Magnus Carlsen wins by being human. *Wall Street Journal.* https://www.wsj.com/articles/magnus-carlsen-ian-nepomniachtchi-world-chess-championship-computer-analysis-11639003641

21. Scarborough, R. C. (2017). Risk a Lot to Save a Lot: How Firefighters Decide Whose Life Matters. *Sociological Forum, 32*(S1), 1073–1092.

22. Ancona, D., & Isaacs, K. (2019, July). How to give your team the right amount of autonomy. Harvard Business Review: https://hbr.org/2019/07/how-to-give-your-team-the-right-amount-of-autonomy.

23. Fox, J. (2014, June 20). Instinct can beat analytical thinking. *Harvard Business Review.* https://hbr.org/2014/06/instinct-can-beat-analytical-thinking; West, D. C., Acar, O. A., & Caruana, A. (2020). Choosing among alternative new product development projects: The role of heuristics. *Psychology & Marketing, 37*(11), 1511–1524.

24. Locke, C. C. (2015, April 30). When it's safe to rely on intuition (and when it's not). *Harvard Business Review*. https://hbr.org/2015/04/when-its-safe-to-rely-on-intuition-and-when-its-not
25. Cohen, D., & Prusak, L. (2001). *In good company: How social capital makes organizations work.* Harvard Business School Press.

Chapter 11

1. Huang, R. (2013, March 14). Six Sigma "killed" innovation at 3M. ZDNet. https://www.zdnet.com/article/six-sigma-killed-innovation-in-3m/
2. Barthelemy, J. (2018, February 27). Why best practices often fall short. *MIT Sloan Management Review*. https://sloanreview.mit.edu/article/why-best-practices-often-fall-short/
3. Barthelemy. (2018, February 27).
4. Baron, J. N., & Hannan, M. T. (2002). Organizational blueprints for success in high-tech start-ups: Lessons from the Stanford Project on Emerging Companies. *California Management Review*, 44(3), 8–36.
5. Authors' interview with Tom Bigda-Peyton, August 31, 2022.
6. Authors' interviews with Don DeGolyer, August 2, 2022, and with Doug Leeby, August 15, 2022.
7. Hinds, P. (2016, June 27). Research: Why best practices don't translate across cultures. *Harvard Business Review*. https://hbr.org/2016/06/research-why-best-practices-dont-translate-across-cultures
8. Dickson, J. (2022, March 28). Sensemaking—The advantage of non-routine leaders. Non Routine Leadership. https://www.nonroutineleadership.com/blog/sensemaking-theadvantageofnonroutineleaders
9. Prahalad, C. K. (2010, April.) Column: Best practices get you only so far. *Harvard Business Review*. https://hbr.org/2010/04/column-best-practices-get-you-only-so-far
10. 60 Minutes. (2020, May 28). From the 60 Minutes archives: J. K. Rowling [Video]. https://www.youtube.com/watch?v=gjWABn5imBw
11. Lawless, J. (2005, Jul. 3). Revealed: The eight-year-old girl who saved Harry Potter. *The Independent*. https://www.independent.co.uk/arts-entertainment/books/news/revealed-the-eightyearold-girl-who-saved-harry-potter-296456.html

12. Ancona, D. (2011). Sensemaking: Framing and acting in the unknown. In S. Snook, N. Nohria, & R. Khurana (Eds.), *The handbook for teaching leadership: Knowing, doing, and being* (pp. 3–16). SAGE.

13. Authors' interview with Mahzer Ahmad, January 20, 2022.

14. Gerstner, L. V. (2002). *Who says elephants can't dance? Inside IBM's historic turnaround.* HarperBusiness.

15. Ancona. (2011).

16. Authors' interview with Josh Lifrak, Dec. 11, 2022.

17. Weick, K.E. (1995). Sensemaking in organizations. Thousand Oaks, CA: Sage Publications.

18. Jaworski, J., & Scharmer, C. (2000). *Leadership in the new economy: Sensing and actualizing emerging futures.* Generon.

19. Ancona, D., Williams, M., & Gerlach, G. (2020, Sep. 8). The overlooked key to leading through chaos. *MIT Sloan Management Review.* https://sloanreview.mit.edu/article/the-overlooked-key-to-leading-through-chaos/

20. Daley, B. J., & Jeris, L. (2004). Boundary spanning. *Advances in Developing Human Resources*, 6(1), 5–8. https://doi.org/10.1177/15234 2230461001

21. Anderson, C. (2012, October 21). Elon Musk's mission to Mars. *Wired.* https://www.wired.com/2012/10/ff-elon-musk-qa/

22. Urban, T. (2015, November 6). The cook and the chef: Musk's secret sauce. Wait But Why. https://waitbutwhy.com/2015/11/the-cook-and-the-chef-musks-secret-sauce.html

23. Ladewig, G. (2008). TRIZ: The theory of inventive problem solving. 10.1002/9780470209943.ch1

24. Melitta. (2013, April 14). Melitta journey through time. https://www.melitta.com/en/Melitta-Journey-through-Time-541.html]

25. MacLellan, L. (2017, September 25). How Microsoft CEO Satya Nadella disrupted the corporate retreat. Quartz. https://qz.com/1086808/how-microsoft-ceo-satya-nadella-disrupted-the-corporate-retreat

Chapter 12

1. Authors' interview with David Bryant, December 6, 2022.

2. Campbell, C. (2023, January 26). Quantum computers could solve countless problems—And create a lot of new ones. *Time.* https://time.com/6249784/quantum-computing-revolution/

Acknowledgments

Similar to the leadership landscape it describes, this book emerged over the course of a long journey of discovery and adaptation, quite different from what we originally planned. It improved over the course of many interactions, big and small, and we appreciate everyone who helped along the way. We're especially grateful to our wives, Haley Garcia and Rachel Fisher, for their tremendous patience and support—they keep us grounded in an unpredictable world. Thanks to everyone at Contemporary Leadership Advisors for picking up the slack. Thanks to our clients, interviewees, and researcher partners for sharing their tremendous stories and insights. Thanks to Marshall Goldsmith for his encouragement and contribution; our collaborators, John Landry and Seth Schulman, for helping to refine the message; our agent, Jud Laghi, for believing in what we had to say; and to everyone at Wiley for making this book a reality. Finally, thanks to our late friend, colleague and business partner, Dr. David Peterson, whose wisdom elevates and inspires us, and whose legacy lives on through the many leaders he coached to excel in complexity and disruption.

About the Authors

Steve Garcia is cofounder and a managing partner at Contemporary Leadership Advisors (CLA), where he helps clients lead faster, more adaptive organizations and higher impact organizations. He is also a cofounder and board member of the Institute for Contemporary Leadership, which brings together executives to explore the future of leadership. Previously, Steve helped run AlixPartners' leadership and organizational effectiveness practice; developed SYNAPP, a people analytics platform acquired by Heidrick & Struggles; led product marketing for Nortel Networks' digital switching, optical Ethernet, and voice-over-IP portfolios, and worked for the US Congress' Office of Technology Assessment.

He holds an MBA from The University of Virginia and an EdD in adult learning from North Carolina State University, where he studied how organizations' informal networks affect learning, change, and innovation. When he's not working, he spends time with his family in New Jersey, catching up on pop culture, and falling down mountains on his bike.

Dan Fisher is also cofounder and a managing partner at CLA, and cofounder and board member of the Institute for Contemporary Leadership. He too previously comanaged the leadership and organizational effectiveness practice at AlixPartners. He works as a trusted leadership advisor to CEOs and their teams, helping them to ensure they have the right players with the right habits and alignment on the right priorities. Prior to working exclusively with senior corporate leaders and their teams, Dan was a clinically trained trauma and forensic psychologist. He gained invaluable lifelong perspective from working as an attending psychologist on New York Hospital's world-renowned Burn Unit and in the New York City Court System.

He holds a PhD in clinical psychology from the University of California, Santa Barbara; a BS in psychology from University of California, San Diego; and completed his postdoctoral studies at Cornell Medical College. More important, he is a proud graduate of the Bronx High School of Science and devoted board member to the amazing nonprofit Row New York. When he's not working, he spends time with his family in New Jersey, works on refining his composting skills, and enjoys acting out his wife's screenplays.

Index